The Glory of A Wasted Life

an adventure with God

christ john otto

GREAT AWAKENING
COMMUNICATIONS
2008

Published by Great Awakening Communications, Inc.
in association with BookSurge Publishing.

ISBN# 1-4392-0675-9

Printed in the United States of America

contents

Throughout human history, there are moments that are pregnant with significance. The moment William the Conqueror won the Battle of Hastings in 1066. The moment they called "don't shoot until you see the whites of their eyes" at Bunker Hill in 1775. The moment Eisenhower and his men stormed the beaches of Normandy.

And throughout human history, there have been moments pregnant with eternal significance. The moment Abraham offered his son Isaac. The moment Moses approached a burning bush. The moment Mary said "yes."

We are currently living in a day and a time when moments of temporal and eternal significance are converging. Today is a day when the course of human events is about to collide with the course of heavenly events and begin the greatest transition in the history of the world. A few wise seers have understood this, and their numbers are growing. The days of "business as usual," of marriage and being given in marriage, of eating and drinking and nice careers are over. Today is the day of loaves and fishes. This is a book about how I chose to waste my life in a time pregnant with significance, in the belief that history is progressing to a logical end. It is my hope that you will read of the glory – and the grief – of one wasted life and choose this path as well.

He Never Fails,

Christ John Otto
Epiphany, 2008
Kansas City, Missouri

Acknowledgements

A wise person once said that if you see a turtle on a fence post, you can be sure he didn't get there by himself. Special thanks to Lyn Davis for her invaluable help throughout this project on finding a "voice" and for assisting in the design of the book. Thank you to Kay Gauder and my friends at Akron Pregnancy Services for your support. Thank you to Tricia Nastycz who gave me feedback with the initial manuscript. I am grateful to Carrie Warburton, whose initial gifts to Belonging House made my laptop a reality, and whose early encouragement helped me actually begin writing. I am especially grateful to Anthony Petrucci at Great Awakening Communications. He walked me through this from the initial concept phase to publication.

With God, all things are possible.

Introduction

There is an army forming. It is an army of men and women who walk with a limp. They have struggled and striven and done the best they can to walk into all that God has called them to. In the face of all of the opposition that the world, the flesh, and the devil could muster, they have continued. Some of them, metaphorically, have plucked out their eyes or cut off their hands in order to enter the kingdom of heaven. Some have chosen to appear foolish, in order to display to the world that God uses the foolish things to confound the wise, the weak things to confound the strong.

God is raising up an army. He is giving them weapons that seem useless from a military perspective. They are being equipped with voices raised in song. They are armed with brushes loaded with paint. Their arsenal includes guitars, violins, and Macs. A few carry notebooks and pencils. They make films and write songs. They are having dreams in the night and seeing visions. They are an army like none that has come before, and they are on the forefront of one of the greatest transitions to occur in human history.

God is doing a new thing. Just like Pentecost, like Paul preaching to Gentiles, the conversion of Rome, and the Protestant Reformation, we are in a time in the Christian Church – and in Western Civilization – when the categories are changing, and the entire expression of Christianity is being transformed.

It has taken me five years to write the book you have before you. In part, because I needed to live out some of the things you see here. In part, because I did not understand parts of what was happening to me personally. Also, in part, because I was still holding onto great chunks of my old categories regarding church. These categories included answers to questions that no one was asking anymore. It took a major life crisis, where I "crashed and burned" to bring me to my knees. In that moment of crisis, I cried out to God for two things. First, that he would give me direction. Second, that I would walk into and fulfill my destiny. The adventure that resulted out of those two prayers became the backbone of this project. In that conversion, I discovered that God was calling me to join his army, an army made of artists, musicians, and creative geniuses. After the horrible struggle, I too developed a limp, much like Jacob after he wrestled with the angel.

My destiny is to prepare a dwelling place for God in the earth. Normally

I refer to this as "building him a throne." I did not know what this meant three years ago. Over the past thirty-six months, bits and pieces of the puzzle have begun to "fit together." I have learned that my struggles with sex and drugs and personal identity were not unique. In fact, to varying degrees these struggles seem to be universally shared by those with creative gifts.

Initially, I set out to write a fictionalized account of my life story. In fact, I nearly completed it. After letting some trusted friends read the work, it became clear that I had missed my initial goal. I also began to realize that although the events of the past laid a foundation for my current life, the last three years contain the message I want to share. This short period also lays the foundation for the goal and mission of my life: to display to the world that God can be trusted, and to raise up an army of artists called to live a life of worship.

I have upset a few of my long-time acquaintances over my recent choices. These choices were based on what I felt was very clear guidance from God. They were also based on a belief that if you do what you love, the money will follow. Finally, they were based on the overwhelming assumption that God is good, and if he guides you, those choices will be good choices. Many people who love me thought I was wasting my time and wasting my life.

I have discovered that out of this experience I have walked into a glorious life. Ministry is no longer difficult or a struggle. I no longer find myself trying to "make connections" or get into the right network. Daily, my life sparkles with the fingerprints of the one who is guiding me, and others are drawn to that sparkle. As John Wesley once said, "get on fire for God, and all the world will come to watch you burn."

This book is an invitation to consider wasting your life. It is an invitation to throw yourself on the mercy of an all-knowing, and all-powerful God who describes himself as "love."

I am sure that some of the things I have written will challenge or maybe even offend you. I have to admit, I was challenged, and at times offended by God while I was walking through the events I describe. There were days when I questioned what was happening, and even wondered if I was crazy. Every time, God continued to confirm what he was doing through multiple sources. And he affirmed me in the process.

It is the hope of this writer that you will keep an open heart as I bear witness to the work of God in my life.

1

one: not so normal

I PLANNED ON HAVING A QUIET CAREER IN A QUIET EPISCOPAL parish in New England. Instead, I was brought to my knees. That humbling brought about something I thought I already had experienced: a conversion. Once my life had been converted, I discovered that God was doing a lot more than I expected. There was something bigger going on, and someone bigger than me involved. About two years ago, I began to see the various themes in my life begin to converge. Through that experience I learned two things, God can be trusted, and that we need to listen to God and do what He tells us.

Both of these points seem pretty simple and straightforward. I spent eight years getting a theological education, and i don't recall having heard them. I have discovered that very few people, myself included, really believe those two things. We doubt that God is good, so we trust our own instincts. And we don't really believe that God knows best for us, so we do what we think is the "common sense" thing to do. To my utter shock, I discovered that common sense is not faith.

I was born in a typical small town in Upstate New York and had a fairly typical life for somebody my age growing up in the 1970's. Springville was a typical northeastern village. Settled right after the Revolution, the town was the result of land grants to veterans from Massachusetts by the Holland Land Company. At first glance, it was built on the blueprint of all small New England towns. A common green served as the hub of all the town's streets. Around the green were planted large maples. In the spring these trees were tapped for their sap, and in the fall they provided hedges waist deep of orange and red fallen leaves. On each side of the green were a church, the town hall, and brick streets. Where cows and sheep once grazed, a large white bandstand presided. With the bandstand there were a monument to "Our Union Dead" and a cannon. The cannon was originally used in times of drought; the sound of the shot was believed to seed rain. By the late 1960's the cannon was aimed directly at a three-story brick apartment building. The residents had little fear of attack, and children were often found sitting on the ancient field gun.

As one walked south along Buffalo Street from the green, they would pass the former Universalist Church, now under the charge of Miss Bensley as the village library. Miss Bensley would serve 62 years as librarian, with as much dignity and respect as Queen Victoria. Main Street was a typical American scene, mostly buildings dating from the 1870's, with one or two clearly federal structures thrown in. The jewel of Main Street was an inn built in the 1860's as a stop for the Pony Express. Out front was an ornate colonnade, and the building was capped by a large cupola. In jarring contrast, in the 1940's a large neon sign was added, reading "The Leland House."

Up the hill to the east was a row of Victorian Mansions; down the road to the west was the Catholic Church as well as many smaller homes owned by mill workers and laborers. West Main had a small delicatessen, an old train depot, and the cemetery. As one left town, there was the auction house, where every Wednesday one could find everything from sheep and cheese to hippies and Amish.

The village was built on the first ridge of hills east of Lake Erie. Because of this location, Springville bore the brunt of heavy snows from late October to early May. The snow and terrain were a boon to skiers, and throughout the winter the village greeted hundreds of Canadians who had come to ski at the surrounding ski resorts. The locals, largely coming from New England stock, greeted these tourists as intruders and made it a point to be cool toward them.

By the early 1970's the town slowly began to experience the aftermath of Woodstock. Hippies and members of the New York counterculture descended on the village and other picturesque hamlets throughout Upstate New York and Vermont. They were looking for cheap rents, inspiring scenery, and freedom from the New York art scene. My home town attracted those who were creative, cynical, and tired of the commercial game. Tired of trying to make it, they wanted to come out from under the orthodoxy of abstract expressionism and do their own thing. Not to mention, grow their own pot.

By stark contrast, the locals held onto traditional small town peculiarity. They didn't even know what "mod" was. Yet, their way of life gave them a deep connection to the earth, an interrelation with her seasons, and profound respect for the power of nature. Because of this, the farmers and the hippies soon experienced a symbiosis. Their two very different ways of life began to intermingle, and they eventually became mutually dependent.

I didn't know it, but I was living in the middle of a cultural revolution. Because this was New York, we were a little ahead of the rest of the country. My parents gave me a lot of options in regard to morality, religion, and career. I was about ten years ahead of most of the "Busters." I didn't know I was postmodern, or that my attitudes and ideas were radical. It was my fishbowl. From birth I was sensitive and artistic, and this exposure to the arts also impacted my perspective on the world.

Unfortunately, many of the adults in my life were not excited about me becoming an artist. The school system could not handle my intense creativity. They were mostly concerned with filling in little black dots on standardized tests.

My kindergarten teacher had contacted the Buffalo Performing Arts Academy about the logistics of sending me to the magnate school for creative and unconventional children. As she explained the possibilities to my parents, they became increasingly uncomfortable. Immediate thoughts of the cost, the trouble of bussing, and the possibility of encouraging the outrageous parts of my personality hit them.

My parents responded to the teacher by telling her "we just want him to be normal." Unfortunately, I wasn't normal. I was creative, artistic and musical, and I read a book a day. From the first grade until the eighth grade, I attempted to fit into a world designed for convention. I never fit in. Then, in the eighth grade, one of my friends invited me to a confirmation class at the Methodist Church.

THE GLORY OF A WASTED LIFE

two: all so new

THE METHODIST CHURCH WAS SOMEWHAT TRAPPED in a time warp from the early seventies. By 1985, Vietnam, the Civil Rights movement, and Watergate were no longer major themes in American society. Unfortunately, the liberal establishment had positioned themselves to be part of the counter-culture that had developed in the nineteen sixties. They "branded" their position with Day-Glo felt banners that pictured butterflies and peace signs. Like the theology they represented, these banners were faded, often missing one or two key components – a letter or two falling off when the Elmer's glue gave way. To kids who were living in the Reagan era, this was a strange contrast. The clergy at the church were committed to a version of the Christian faith that was void of miracles, heavy on social justice, and uncomfortable with some of the claims of orthodox doctrine. To their credit, the church was full of faithful Christians who quietly prayed and waited for the next minister to be appointed to their charge.

To this world where the coming theological storms had not yet blown, I wandered. I had really never been in church before, and was immediately gripped by the holiness of the place. I was drawn to the altar where my parents were married and to the font where I had been baptized. I did not know much about Christianity, so it was all new and all interesting. I had not heard the sermons that everyone else in the room had heard.

As Elizabeth Barrett Browning once wrote:

"Every bush is aflame with God.

Only those who see it take off their shoes.

The rest of us sit around and eat blackberries."

I did not know that the Book said one thing, but that most of the people believed something else. I had not sat in the church and heard the preacher say,

"Now Jesus didn't really mean that." I took the words in the Bible to mean what they said. I was a voracious reader, and figured that you read the Bible like every other book. I didn't know any better.

Up to this point, I had very little religious training, and found it fascinating. I was not astute enough yet to recognize some of the jargon, and accepted it all. Even though the class was heavy on church membership rules and denominational politics, there was enough Bible to catch my attention – enough Bible to cause me to spend extra curricular time reading the New Testament.

One Sunday afternoon, my parents decided it was a fine time to be alone, and called my grandmother to see if she could keep their boy for the afternoon. That afternoon, I took my homework, my drawing books, and an old Bible to my grandmother's house.

That afternoon I wasn't interested in spending time with the adults, but my grandparents had invited some guests for dinner. Among these was a woman who radiated life and joy. Her face positively glowed. I didn't know it, but I had met this woman several years earlier, and at that time she was anything but healthy. She had been grey and ragged before. At the time of our previous meeting she was an alcoholic, a prescription drug addict, and had been diagnosed with cancer. On top of that, she smoked – a lot. In the time that had passed, she had been transformed. She was energetic, animated, and was "glowing" with life.

"Jesus has done amazing things in my life!" She dominated the dinner conversation and the after-dinner conversation. In fact, she broke all the rules of a northeastern household and talked about her religion.

"You know, I was dying, and I prayed. You know what happened? I'll tell you what happened. Jesus came and healed me. I held out my hand to him. My arm was full of tumors, you know — and he came and healed me. I felt this amazing heat, and then the tumors were gone!"

I had never heard anything like this before. I sat mesmerized as she recounted how she quit using drugs, stopped drinking, and gave up smoking. Grandma kept trying to change the subject, but no matter what topic they chose, the lady kept coming back to Jesus.

After dinner, while Grandma was in the kitchen doing dishes, we talked about the confirmation class and what I had been reading in the Bible.

"You know, you can know Jesus too." The guest reached out her hand to me, I took it.

"Yes, but how? I have never heard any of this before." I was a little surprised in her offer. My family did not talk about these matters. My exposure to religion was all so new, and I wasn't sure what to do.

"Let me see your Bible." She opened up the Bible to page 1066 and read it to me.

"Unless you are born again, you cannot see the Kingdom of God."

"What does that mean?" Now things were really confusing.

"If you say 'yes' to Jesus, then you will be born again. You get a new life. Everything is wiped clean and you can start over. That's what happened to me. Do you want to be born again?"

I thought for a moment, and as I thought, my heart began to pound. I didn't realize all the implications of the lady's question. I had not pondered all that would be asked of me in the future. I didn't understand who was calling me, but I knew that someone beyond the middle-aged dinner guest was reaching out to me. I was being given an opportunity, and as a child, I responded. I nodded my head.

"Then let me pray for you." As she grabbed my hand, I felt something that was new to me. It felt something like electricity but was much warmer and more soothing. As she prayed, the feeling became more intense. By the time she was done, Grandma came back into the room. She wasn't sure what had been going on, but she guessed there was some evangelizing that had taken place — right under her nose.

That night, as she took me home, she looked me in the eyes and coolly remarked:

"It's alright to have beliefs, but it is never proper to push them off on anybody else."

A deep fear came over me, and I never talked about what happened with anyone in my family.

The first few months after becoming a Christian were glorious. Every day I spent hours reading the new Bible that I was given at Confirmation. The book seemed alive, and the pages seemed loaded with new things that were full of a three-dimensional reality. Most exciting was what the Bible said about prayer.

"Ask anything in my name, and I will do it."

"Ask, seek, and knock."

Within weeks I was praying for things. I prayed for new clothes. I prayed for food for my family. I prayed for the weather. I prayed that I would do better in school. My parents weren't sure what had happened, but they were grateful for the change.

I found ways to get out of the house now, too. And through hanging out at the small religious bookstore downtown, I had begun to meet a number of the local religious nuts. I listened to people talk about books they were reading, discussed doctrine, and met new people. From these contacts, I picked up odd jobs in the community.

My parents were beginning to get a little annoyed with the turn my life was taking. They couldn't figure out why I was so religious.

three: open your mouth

MY PARENTS REALLY DIDN'T KNOW WHAT WAS GOING ON. They thought I had joined a cult. Throughout my teenage years, while my friends were experimenting with sex and drugs, I was getting up to go to 6 a.m. prayer meetings, and going to Billy Graham crusades. I stopped attending the Methodist Church in 1987, and began attending another smaller church in Springville. It was nothing like the church I had been going to. They had a band. A rock band with drums, guitars, bass, and a grinding Hammond organ. They projected the words to the songs on the wall with an overhead projector. Everyone clapped when they sang, and raised their hands.

They also had a colorful, flamboyant pastor named Tim Mather. Tim had been known to preach a sermon in his pajamas and bathrobe or jump up onto the communion rail. Most of all, New Life Fellowship was disliked because it drew crowds. Their Sunday school attendance was larger than the entire Baptist church. They were starting to impact the other churches as members came for a visit out of curiosity, and never returned to their previous parish. Most of the folks in town had never been to a church where things actually happened.

One morning, something unusual happened.

After the collection, Pastor Tim stood up.

"How many of you are born-again?" the preacher shouted. A majority, including myself, raised their hands.

"How many of you are filled with the Holy Spirit?"

Once again, a large number of the church raised their hands.

"Today, I am going to tell you how to be filled with the Holy Ghost!"

With that, Tim launched into a dramatic sermon retelling the events at the beginning of the book of Acts. With vivid descriptions, he painted a portrait of the apostles huddled waiting in the upper room. With increasing intensity, the people responded to the preacher's sermon.

"And they waited for the Promise of the Father."

"Amen!"

"They waited and prayed."

"Uh-huh!"

"They waited for days and nights."

As the sermon built to the climax, the moment when the tongues of fire appeared, the wind blew, and the house shook, Pastor Tim had brought the church to the moment of decision.

"Do you want to be filled with the Holy Ghost?"

"Yes!"

"Do you want to be baptized with the Spirit and with Power?"

"Yes!"

"Then come on down, and we will pray for you."

The band began to play; the people began to sing; and I got up out of my seat.

Approaching the front, I knelt down at the simple padded rail. I wasn't sure what was about to happen, but I was hungry for what these folks had. Eventually, the small team praying for those who had come forth approached me.

"Now, son," an older man knelt down and looked me in the eye. "We are going to lay hands on you and you are going to be filled with the Holy Spirit. You are going to feel the Holy Spirit fill you from the bottom of your feet to the top of your head."

I nodded. They dabbed oil on my forehead, and the small group gathered around me and put their hands on my shoulders and head. Then, almost immediately, something strange, but not frightening, began to happen. I heard the people around me begin to pray in what seemed like Chinese or Arabic. Another person sounded like Hindi. Although the languages were interesting, I was soon captivated by the physical sensation overtaking my body. It was like the night at my grandmother's dining room table, only much stronger. I felt as if I were being charged with massive amounts of electricity; only they were comforting, cleansing waves rather than shocks.

From that moment on, something was radically different in my life. The Bible took on a different tone. Things seemed to be written in neon, and they leapt off the page. My artwork took on a new quality. I began to get involved in music, and began to play the piano. I started being involved in music in school, but soon this transferred into church. I was having an amazing time.

I was still wondering about the languages.

While riding my bike down a country road, I quietly prayed, "God, if you want me to speak in tongues, I will."

That night I went to bed. It wasn't a particularly unusual night. It had been a particularly average day. But, at about three o'clock in the morning, I was awakened by something. More specifically, Someone awakened me.

"Christ, get on your knees and pray."

I obeyed the instruction, whether it was a thought in my head, or an audible sound. As I prayed, my prayer became praise. As I began to praise God, the words I used became unfamiliar. Then I began to sing, and pour out my soul to the One who had roused me from sleep. I didn't understand what was happening, or the tremendous peace that began to flow over me. One thing was clear: my life was changed. I was no longer merely a Christian. A portal had opened up that connected me to God in a whole new way.

As the weeks of the summer progressed and waned toward fall, so did these nighttime prayer sessions. I would awake around three, pray for an hour or so, and then return to bed.

One night in August, I was again awakened by the voice in the night.

"Christ, open your Bible and begin to read."

The leaves of my Bible fell open to the following passage:

And He said to me: "Son of man, I am sending you to the children of Israel, to a rebellious nation that has rebelled against Me; they and their fathers have transgressed against Me to this very day. For they are impudent and stubborn children. I am sending you to them, and you shall say to them, 'Thus says the Lord GOD.' As for them, whether they hear or whether they refuse, for they are a rebellious house, yet they will know that a prophet has been among them.

And you, son of man, do not be afraid of them nor be afraid of their words, though briers and thorns are with you and you dwell among scorpions; do not be afraid of their words or dismayed by their looks, though they are a rebellious house. You shall speak My words to them, whether they hear or whether they refuse, for they are rebellious. But you, son of man, hear what I say to you. Do not be rebellious like that rebellious house; open your mouth and eat what I give you." (Ezekiel 2:3-8, NKJV).

After that, I heard the voice say to me, "This is for you." Then I went back to bed.

The next morning I went to see my pastor. Pastor Tim counseled me to begin looking for a solid Christian college to attend, and to begin getting as much education as possible. This was a radical change of plans for me because I had been planning on attending the Art Institute of Pittsburgh and getting a degree in commercial art. Instead, I enrolled in Houghton College.

In 1848, a farmer-turned preacher looked down from a high hill on a little village below. Jockey Street, as the place was called, was a resting place on the Erie Canal, just beyond the reach of the law. Since it was an unincorporated settlement, there were no sheriff, no mayor, and no village council. Just a collection of rambling houses and buildings forming makeshift brothels, gin mills, and gambling parlors.

Willard J. Houghton was a holiness preacher who built a little chapel in the town. Atop its steeple, he placed a carved hand, one finger pointing upward toward heaven. This sign, ignored by the villagers, was a reminder of the higher purpose in the town's existence.

Sunday after Sunday, Willard preached in his chapel, to his family and a couple farmers who were brave enough to come into the disreputable town. Daily, he would climb the hill overlooking the town and pray. In frustration, he would get on his knees, lift up his eyes to God, and cry out:

"Oh God, make this place a place more known for holiness than it is for vice!"

Soon, civilization would reach the frontier – so would trains.

Almost one hundred and fifty years later, my parents drove up a long winding road to a school on the hill overlooking the remains of Jockey Street. They were taking me to the physical result of that impassioned prayer. Houghton College was an academically astute Christian liberal arts school tucked in the hills of Upstate New York.

The air was crisp in early fall when I moved my things into the dormitory. I met a number of other freshmen, all from a variety of places in the northeast. For the first time, I was in a "Christian" environment.

Somewhere in the time between high school and college, I also accepted the idea that the visual arts were not acceptable for a Christian. I laid aside my gifts, and focused on music — a medium acceptable for a Christian. At the time, many in the church were teaching a lot about the making of "graven images" and avoiding idolatry.

The four years I spent at Houghton were especially formative because of

"Coach" George Wells, a retired professor who led a ministry called Youth in One Accord. Coach and the "team" traveled to small churches throughout the northeastern United States and presented revival meetings. I learned a lot about character, integrity, and service through the work we did. Often, it was hard. Coach demanded a high level of accountability among the team, especially in the area of interpersonal relationships. We were required to keep an open relationship with our fellow team members. More than once we experienced a tear-filled time of reconciliation and forgiveness before we went out to minister. For the first time, I saw what I would call a real revival happen in one of these weekends off campus.

One time in particular, we were singing at a church near Syracuse, New York. It was a Southern Baptist mission that was meeting in a converted warehouse. At first, it didn't seem like a very remarkable location or meeting. Our typical routine was to sing a song, then share a short impromptu testimony between each song. After twenty or so minutes of this program, Coach would preach. This morning, one of the testimonies impacted the pastor.

I don't believe Coach preached that morning, but rather opened the meeting for the congregation to come forward for prayer. The first one in the front was the pastor. This meeting went on late into the afternoon, and we left the church around supper time. To be there, it seemed as though time had stopped, and only a few moments had lapsed.

My on-campus experience at Houghton was very different. The students on campus were largely from wealthy east coast families who, although from evangelical churches, were not deeply spiritual. Because of this, I soon began to pray for a revival at the school. Many of my classmates acted as if they had no Christian faith at all. My core group of friends joined this movement of prayer for the student body. We wanted to see something happen that would change lives, and change our school.

A "revival" is the term traditionally used to describe a resurgence of religious passion and fervor. Charles Finney first used the term in the early 19th century. Generally, revivals are marked by an initial awareness of sin and lukewarmness among Christians. This results in Christians' turning from sinful activities, making a renewed commitment to God, and having a new experience with the Holy Spirit. In the initial stages, revivals tend to have a heightened emotional quality, often accompanied by extended meetings, spontaneous singing, miracles, physical manifestations, and mystical experiences. All the great revivals in history soon impacted the larger society with mass conversions to Christianity. This resulted in massive social change. Examples of this happening include the Evangelical Revival (1739-50) under John and Charles Wesley in England, the First and Second Great Awakenings in America, and the Welsh Revival of 1906.

The "something" for which we were praying actually happened during my senior year. Every semester began with a "Christian Life Emphasis Week." The C.L.E.W. was a more palatable version of the old time revival meetings that the school held in its more fundamentalistic past. Most semesters the meetings were lectures on theological topics, opening with special music by each student body class. This semester, the guest preacher came and began talking about sin, about surrendering your life to the control of Jesus Christ, and about the call to a life of holiness. The response among the students was overwhelming. The rest of the semester was marked by a real change in the culture at the school.

For me personally, the speaker, Jimmy Johnson, said something that had a profound impact, and set the tone for the rest of my life. I don't remember much of what he said, but I remember these instructions. He said, "If you really want to follow God, go back to your room. Take out a piece of white typing paper and then sign the bottom of the paper. That blank piece of paper will serve as a contract between you and God. From that moment on, God will fill in the rest." That night I went home and took out a piece of paper. I signed and dated it.

That's when my life began to go into the toilet.

four: no one is asking

IN MY LATE TEENS I BEGAN TO STRUGGLE with same sex attraction. I kept
this secret, and even dated girls in college. Although the term "gay" was in use,
homosexuality was not talked about that much in the late eighties. AIDS was
on the TV, but people thought of that as something "out there" in San
Francisco or New York. After graduating from Houghton, I discovered the
school had had a small homosexual subgroup led by a resident director in one
of the dorms. I did share with some of my close friends the feelings and internal
struggle I was experiencing, but largely I kept things to myself. I was a good
Christian, a leader on campus, and headed for seminary.

After I gave God permission to have control over my life, this quiet
struggle with homosexuality began to get stronger. Like a smelter, the heat was
rising to reveal the hidden impurities in my soul. I left Houghton in June 1993,
and two weeks later, began summer Greek at Asbury Theological Seminary.

I visited Asbury the first week of April, when it was still winter in New
York. Kentucky was beginning to come alive with dogwoods, redbuds, and
foals in the fields. Springtime in Kentucky is magical. The grass takes on a blue
tinge, and the sky is dotted with little cottony clouds. Woodford County, just
west of Lexington, relished rituals cultivated before the Civil War. White gloved
and hatted ladies met jacketed men for meets at Keeneland. Afternoon socials
with julep cups where white fences along tree-lined lanes led to antebellum
mansions. Romantic and ridiculous, genteel and barbarous, refined and
scandalous, Kentucky cast a spell on many visitors. I was hexed on my visit.

Asbury was founded by a fire-breathing holiness preacher named Henry
Clay Morrison. The school that bore his name grew out of an extended stay at
the Wilmore Camp Meeting in the 1890s. I was drawn to Asbury because it had

a long history of promoting revival. Unlike Houghton, Asbury had an understanding of holiness grounded in rule-keeping and separation from the world. By the time I arrived, most of the "holier than thou" attitude had been suppressed, but it was still deep in the DNA of the school and its surrounding community. Asbury still held a rigidly interpreted code of conduct that forbade smoking, drinking, dancing, and sex. By sharp contrast, within the surrounding territory of the school property could be found horse racing, tobacco fields, a bourbon distillery, and cock fighting. By the early 1990's, Asbury was embracing a softened image that embraced respectability and recognition. Asbury had made its goal the United Methodist Church – to take over and transform it.

The first few days in Wilmore were especially difficult. Suddenly, I began to have serious anxiety problems. Most nights, I remained awake in bed and looked at the ceiling. I went into culture shock. I didn't have many friends. Greek demanded eight hours of studying every day. My support system at Houghton was gone. Then, toward the middle of that first summer, I was befriended by a student a year ahead of me.

What I naively thought was an innocent friendship was, in reality, the beginning of a homosexual relationship. We became roommates, and by mid-fall, we were bedmates.

I wish I could say that I was the victim of an older student taking advantage of me. In truth, I was dealing with a huge amount of pain. All I wanted was someone to hold me. At night, I would rock back and forth and cry out to God, asking him to hold me.

God didn't answer the prayer the way I wanted.

For the next two years, I became the master of the double life. My roommate became a leader on campus, and I secretly dealt with the guilt and shame of my life.

At the same time, I was having a lot of struggles in my classes. Early in the first semester, I was "pegged" by a number of my classmates as a liberal because I asked hard questions. One day in class, I sat at my desk and listened to another lecture on some aspect of Protestant theology. In the margin of my notebook, I made a telling note:

"These people are answering questions no one is asking."

By the end of two years, my roommate went off to Oklahoma. He was ordained in the United Methodist Church, and I was left with the shattered pieces of my life.

Like a lot of Christians involved in sexual sin, I didn't want to give up the sexual activity, and I didn't want to go to hell. As a result, I walked a tightrope between periodic sexual falls and active Christian involvement. I wasn't alone. There were about a dozen fellow students and a couple professors from the seminary that I encountered in local gay bars, dance clubs, and porn shops. We kept each other's secrets, knowing that we would be excused from life at Asbury in a graceless and public way. The evangelical community seemed to "wink and nod" at marital infidelity, pornography, and divorce, but attacked homosexuality as an abomination.

One day, in a real moment of despair, I walked out to the hill behind Asbury. I sat in the grass and quietly wept. It was a windy day, and the grass whipped. I was the most alone I had ever been. There was no one to turn to. At that moment, as if a distant memory had been recalled, I heard something in the wind.

"Do you want to be healed?"

At first, I thought the voice was my imagination. I had all but given up the idea that God could talk to me.

"Do you want to be healed?" Again, the voice echoed on the wind.

"Christ, do you want to be healed?"

Through my tears, I whispered a half-hearted "yes."

"I am going to give you the steps. I promise that you will be healed."

I was still not certain if the voice I heard was my imagination, my thoughts, or the wind. But I was in a desperate state. The loneliness and despair that I felt when first moving to Kentucky had returned, and I had no way to dispel it.

"Christ, go meet with Steve Seamands. He will help you."

That afternoon, I called Dr. Seamands, and made an appointment for the following Wednesday.

"So, Christ, how can I help you?" Steve was warm and compassionate.

"I have been struggling with homosexuality." Those words began an avalanche of emotion and for about fifteen minutes I began to unload all the guilt and the shame I had been bearing for the previous two years. I broke down.

After Steve let me regain my composure, he asked me if there was any more. At that moment, I had told him as much has I knew. Then Dr. Seamands took a small bottle from his bookshelf.

"Christ, I am going to sprinkle you with a little of this blessed water. I have heard your confession, and in the name of Jesus Christ, you are forgiven."

He poured a small amount of the water into his hand, and let it trickle down over my head and shoulders. At that moment, I felt clean. The holy water removed the first layer of schmutz. I felt a relief that I had not known before in my life. Without control, I began to smile.

After a brief prayer, Steve asked me if I had ever read a book by Leanne Payne called *Restoring the Christian Soul Through Healing Prayer.* I hadn't.

"I think you ought to go get it and read it. You have just begun the first few steps of a very long journey. Call me if you need anything."

I left the office feeling lighter and freer than I could ever remember. Something had happened in that little office. At the moment, I wasn't entirely sure what, but I knew that something had changed. If a little something had changed, then a lot more could change. Maybe there was a way out of the confusion and compulsion that had controlled my sexual impulses. Maybe there was hope.

The next day I went to the library to see if I could find the book, but didn't have any luck. Then I went to the bookstore. They didn't carry it, but they could special order it. In a few weeks, the book arrived. I was excited about this "how-to" book on healing. I figured that if I worked through the book in the summer, I could be healed by the following fall.

Reality set in within the first few pages. I didn't understand what Leanne Payne was talking about. She said there were three obstacles to healing: the failure to forgive others, the failure to forgive one's self, and the failure to come into self-acceptance (Payne, 1996). I understood not being able to forgive myself, and not forgiving others. But as for self-acceptance, I didn't even know what that meant.

Within a few months, the initial elation from my first encounter with Dr. Seamands wore off. Bit by bit, the nasty habits returned. I would once again begin to access porn. I would go out for late night drives, and now and again I would meet another man looking to release the same pressures. This was all done quietly. And quietly, the guilt and shame returned. Along with this returned my need to try harder to make the problem go away. I figured if I was a little more disciplined, and a little more controlled, if I had a little more accountability, and read a few more books, I would change. Instead, the fires of homosexuality only intensified, creating a cycle that would repeat again and again.

By the fall, I had met a guy who lived in Cincinnati. I began driving up there on weekends off. David was a little older, and was church going, although not religious. I was tired of the seminary. I was tired of trying harder, and had returned to much the same place I was before meeting with Steve Seamands in the summer. This time was different though.

After my first appointment with Steve, I had begun to tell a number of my friends what had happened. A number of them knew about the initial healing that I had experienced. My earlier affair depended on ignorance and secrecy. Now my closest friends were aware of the signs that I might be acting on my inclinations. A few friends knew that I would go out at night. They were beginning to recognize that I was pulling away from the seminary life.

One afternoon in early January, my phone rang. It was Dr. Seamands.

"Christ, would you be able to come by my office tomorrow?"

"Sure, that should be no problem." I didn't ask what the appointment was about.

The next day I met him in his office.

"I called you in today because your friends wanted me to ask you about your friend in Cincinnati."

At first I was stunned, but then I recognized I was being confronted.

"I want to help you walk this out, Christ. You came here in the summer thinking that this would be a quick and easy change. I don't know everything about homosexuality, but I am willing to walk with you through this as far as I can. Why don't we meet every two weeks, and see what happens."

I agreed to meet with Steve every two weeks. The combination of emotions I felt was overwhelming. A group of my friends had been meeting to plan an intervention. The most compassionate of the group, an old friend from Houghton, Cindy Fox, encouraged them to ask Steve to confront me. She knew that if the whole group did it, I would drop out of school. She was right.

Around this time I was reading a book by Dr. Frank Lake, entitled Clinical Theology. Something in the writing triggered a series of memories that were pretty traumatic. The first memories were overwhelming. After a few weeks, I dropped all but one of my classes. The emotional strain of the turmoil I was experiencing made it impossible for me to work.

The dark images continued for several weeks. First, there were the penises, coming at me out of the dark. Then there were memories of dark figures in the night. Faceless, these forms came at me and attacked me. I didn't remember much more. But with the images came rage like I had never known. The memories made me feel as if I were a house where the electrical system had short-circuited or blitzed out. I was experiencing the emotions of a three-

THE GLORY OF A WASTED LIFE

year-old, only I was twenty-three. I felt out of control, violated, dirty, and powerless. At night my heart would race. I would see the forms in the dark, and be passive in the face of them. Sometimes I would remember sounds, odors, and feelings. Mostly I remembered the dark.

One afternoon I was feeling almost catatonic from the pain and anxiety. I went to visit a friend in Lexington, and crashed on her couch. As the pain increased, I lay back on her couch and closed my eyes. I began to quietly pray. When I opened them, I saw on the wall a moving hand-carved crucifix. As I looked at the image of the Redeemer, I heard that familiar, still small voice in my soul.

"See, Christ, I can take it. I can take it all if you give it to me."

At first, I wasn't sure what to do, but I listened.

"Christ, I can take all of the pain, all of the anger, I can take the rage, give it to me."

I felt the effects of the abuse coming to the surface. They looked like great blotches of red. I saw them go into Jesus' body on the cross. The red rage I experienced went into the scarlet blood flowing from the corpus.

"That's right, Christ. I can take it. There is nothing that you are experiencing that I can't handle. I have suffered all abuse, shame and pain, so you do not have to. I will bear it for you."

That afternoon I discovered the practical application of the theological concepts that I had learned in school. What was doctrine became a vital reality in the face of the misery I was living. I later discovered that I had experienced a psychological breakthrough. Next week, I met with Dr. Seamands, and we discussed what happened. He was thrilled with the news.

"Now, Christ, can you take it a step further? Can you forgive the person who abused you?"

I agreed, prayed and said the words that I forgave the perpetrator. It would be about six more years before I was able to "walk out" that forgiveness, but it was the first step. I didn't feel anything. That session concluded with a simple communion service in Dr. Seamands' office.

That night I was able to think clearly for the first time in several months. I was also able to begin doing my school work again. Within the next few weeks, I was able to get caught up and complete my incomplete work.

five: going opposite directions

AROUND THIS TIME, TWO INTERESTING DEVELOPMENTS OCCURRED. I began to take on a lot of freelance art work, mostly textile work for churches. The struggles I had were awakening my gifts from a self-imposed dormancy. I also began to attend a small Vineyard Church in Kentucky. Each week I would go to the incredibly informal church and would close my eyes. When I did, I saw myself in priest's vestments, leading a dance around the altar. Then I would hear the words "wandering Episcopalian." At the time, I was attending a healing service at a local Episcopal church. Beyond that, I felt that the Episcopal Church was too "liberal" for me. I couldn't see myself attending the Episcopal Church without being involved somewhere else. At the same time, I was attracted to the liturgy, to the pageantry, and to the openness toward the arts and artists.

That spring I began attending Christ Church Cathedral with some friends. Christ Church was self-consciously historic. Brass plates memorialized their illustriously deceased members. It was the "de facto church" of the horse industry, and counted some famous horse farms among its membership. On the surface the parish was conservative and comfortable. They boasted the best music in the city, and one of the best choirs in the country. I was drawn to the fact that I could go and kneel and pray, and no one would speak to me or demand that I make some emotional response. I needed solace and comfort. The church's entrenched Episcopalianism offered just that. Here I was with Pentecostal roots, holiness training, and evangelical foundations taking refuge among the sleepy mink coats and needlepoint kneelers.

I decided to keep myself on the fringe of life at the cathedral. I enjoyed the sermons that were intellectually stimulating, uplifting, and for the most part, orthodox. The liturgy, in its quaint Elizabethan English, provided me with the most support. Into the mix was the ethereal music, giving me an aesthetic fix that carried me through the week.

Somehow I got on a list for confirmation at Easter 1996. I decided to go through with it. By the fall, I was involved in starting a new mission church for the Episcopal Diocese of Lexington — Church of the Apostles. The young priest of the church invited me to make a three-year commitment to help start the church. In exchange, he would help me get into the ordination process. On paper, this sounded like a tidy arrangement. In reality, the unwritten rules, the personalities, and the political agendas involved made it a minefield.

Early on, I discovered that I would have to, at the very least, lie about my personal convictions to get ordained. It also became clear that trying to leave the homosexual lifestyle was not the position of the diocese. I was too open and made a few mistakes with key "players" in the diocese. I was just getting used to listening to God, and no one had told me that you should keep those things to yourself and learn to discern what was God and what was your own brokenness.

In the end, my priest backed away and let me hang. Homosexuality was becoming a litmus test in the church for new clergy, and a few churches were already beginning to leave the denomination by the late 1990's. I was trying to walk out of homosexuality, while the Episcopal Church was diving deeper into it. We were on the same road, going in opposite directions.

I stayed in Lexington three years after seminary. During that time, it felt like the ground I had gained with Dr. Seamands was lost, or at least strongly eroded. I still struggled, and tried to manage my sexual activity. Unfortunately, I lived in a city where many prominent citizens were doing the same thing I was. In my late night excursions, I met priests, doctors, lawyers, politicians, and TV personalities.

I knew I needed a change, but I didn't know how to make it. I had left the Church of the Apostles where I was working - burned out and broken. On Sundays, out of duty, I would go to big churches and sit in the back pew and leave early.

In the late summer, a good friend suggested that I attend a conference at St. Luke's Episcopal Church in Akron, Ohio. St. Luke's was a renegade church that was involved in the "Charismatic Renewal." Emotional music, speaking in tongues, and prayer for healing marked their church. St. Luke's was also deeply committed to ministry with men and women who wanted to leave homosexuality behind. Most of this ministry was through leading a program called "Living Waters." I needed to get away, and this seemed like the ideal place to go.

In October 1999, I drove up to Akron, and stayed the weekend. Something happened to me that weekend. For the first time, I saw a church where the arts, dynamic spirituality, and the ritual that marks the Episcopal Church were married. I felt as though I had found a home.

After driving back to Lexington, I decided I would drive back to Akron for church the next Sunday. Leaving Kentucky at 4:30 in the morning, I would arrive just in time for church. At the time, gas was pretty cheap, so I could afford the trip. I continued driving five hours to church every Sunday for the next six weeks. By late November, I decided to move to Ohio.

The move to Akron was not smooth. In the first three weeks, I was thrown out of the house where I was staying because I was still going out at night looking for sexual encounters. Eventually, I settled in my own apartment. For a year I took several temporary jobs. It was a great year of healing. If the church doors were open, I went in. At the time, St. Luke's hosted internationally known speakers, and something was happening every Sunday. I also became part of a great small group.

Unfortunately, I was still obsessed with becoming a priest. As I was getting healed, the direction of the Episcopal Church was becoming more and more committed to sanctioning homosexuality. But I was hungry for a career in the church. After a year, I took a job at St. Luke's, in hopes that I would become a priest. Instead, I worked hard – very hard. It was 2001, and in September the attack on New York resulted in a drop in all charitable giving. The rector called me in and let me go, saying that there was no budget for my position. I had spent the year cleaning up messes for the ordained clergy, and in the end I was fired. I was pretty angry, and decided to let people know.

As I mentioned before, there were many unwritten rules in the ordination process. I had learned that the Episcopal Church functioned like a private boys club. The ordination process and the seminary program were a closed system that resulted in loyalty among the clergy.

Working at St. Luke's, I learned that I had broken one of the unspoken rules among clergy. A person who goes to seminary without a bishop's permission is considered a troublemaker. Most of my experience with clergy was colored by this perception, even though I was nearly finished with seminary when I began working in the Episcopal Church. Such was the case at St. Luke's. The priests on staff at the time were absent most of the time, and it fell to me and another lay seminary graduate on staff to handle most of the pastoral emergencies.

In my anger for being let go, I decided I was going to tell key members of the parish what was happening. In exchange for silence, the rector of St. Luke's agreed to put me in an ordination process. It would not be announced to the congregation, and St. Luke's would contribute no money to the expense (several thousand dollars). Essentially, this was a vote of no confidence on his part. One of many I had received. I was the bastard son.

I was given three months to find another job. My search ended when I took a job at a large United Methodist Church in Orlando, Florida. For the first time, my connections from Asbury worked in my favor. They offered me an incredible salary and benefits package, and there would be enough money to meet my ordination expenses and get caught up on my student loans. I jumped at the job. Of course, I was in a very rocky place personally. St. Luke's was "propping" me up, and I was really not as healthy as I thought. The move to Florida removed these props, and within days of being in Orlando, I was back to the old habit of living a double life.

In desperation, I looked for someone to give me help. I found a local "ex-gay" ministry, and began to meet with the director. I was experiencing internal chaos. As I look back, God was removing all the things in my life that I used to prevent me from getting "real" about the struggle I was facing. Outwardly, I was the uber-Christian, and inwardly I was conflicted between meeting my sexual desires and fulfilling the call God had on my life. The job in Florida was great, but I lacked the community that I had experienced in Akron. Part of me really wanted to do whatever I needed to do to get through the struggle. My friend at the ex-gay ministry encouraged me to tell the pastor of the church what I was going through. I agreed, and confessed my recent sexual falls.

At the time, I thought the meeting went well. In fact, he confessed that he too had struggles with pornography and sexual addiction. My impression was that they would give me a review after a few months probation, and we would see how I was doing.

Unfortunately, about that time, the Roman Catholic clergy sex abuse scandals hit the papers. A week later, I was called into the office of the pastor. He and the assistant minister accused me of being a child molester. They gave me twenty-four hours to clean out my office and one month's pay. Within a few weeks, I discovered that rumors were circulating that I was a gay activist and that I had come there to infiltrate their conservative congregation. In truth, these lies were to cover up the confession that I had heard.

For the first time in my life, I felt like I had nothing to live for. All of the work that I had done, the years of counseling, and the internal struggle all seemed in vain. The hopes of ordination were over. I had to tell my family what happened. I was alone in a strange city. I gave up. My dirty little secret was out, and every one would now know that I was a hypocrite.

For the next three years, I bounced from one bad job to another. I moved every three months or so, dependent on friends to give me a place to stay. My best friends from Asbury, Craig and Dionne Hammond, helped me as best they could. Truthfully, they couldn't help me because I didn't want help.

During this period, I had only one goal – to die.

I wanted to end my life, and have as much pleasure as I could doing it. For the next few years, I got involved in the darkest part of the gay scene in Florida. I began using crystal meth and disappearing for days at a time. Again and again, I encountered guys like me, who had once been in ministry, who were now into the scene. It was dark, and I saw and participated in some horrible things.

My day of reckoning came early in September of 2004. That was the day I discovered I was HIV positive. My goal of suicide was working. With no money, I had no way to pay for the medical treatment I was going to need. I didn't plan on telling anyone. Anyone, that is, except my priest.

Through all of this, I was attending church, and I began driving two hours to All Saints' Church in Winter Park, Florida to attend their healing services. Somewhere down inside I guess I still was hoping for a miracle, or at least for some of the pain to stop. Once a week, I at least received a little comfort. Comfort is what All Saints gave me.

One week I made an appointment with Father Al Durrance. He was a retired priest who wore red socks under his Birkenstocks and did needlepoint to pass the time while talking with people. He had a no-nonsense attitude. Nothing I said shocked him. Father Al gave me some advice that changed my life. At the moment I didn't realize it, but I had experienced a conversion.

"You have problems that are too big for me to handle," he said. "But I know who can handle them. Listen to the Lord, and do what he tells you, and eventually you will get through this." He absolved me, and instructed me to read Romans, chapter 8:

There is therefore now no condemnation for those who are in Christ Jesus. For the law of the Spirit of life in Christ Jesus has set me free from the law of sin and death. For God has done what the law, weakened by the flesh, could not do: sending his own Son in the likeness of sinful flesh and for sin, he condemned sin in the flesh, in order that the just requirement of the law might be fulfilled in us, who walk not according to the flesh but according to the Spirit. For those who live according to the flesh set their minds on the things of the flesh, but those who live according to the Spirit set their minds on the things of the Spirit. To set the mind on the flesh is death, but to set the mind on the Spirit is life and peace. For the mind that is set on the flesh is hostile to God; it does not submit to God's law, indeed it cannot; and those who are in the flesh cannot please God. But you are not in the flesh, you are in the Spirit, if in fact the Spirit of God dwells in you. Any one who does not have the Spirit of Christ does not belong to him.

But if Christ is in you, although your bodies are dead because of sin, your spirits are alive because of righteousness. If the Spirit of him who raised Jesus from the dead dwells in you, he who raised Christ Jesus from the dead will give life to your mortal bodies also through his Spirit which dwells in you. So then, brethren, we are debtors, not to the flesh, to live according to the flesh—for if you live according to the flesh you will die, but if by the Spirit you put to death the deeds of the body you will live. For all who are led by the Spirit of God are sons of God. For you did not receive the spirit of slavery to fall back into fear, but you have received the spirit of sonship. When we cry, "Abba! Father!" it is the Spirit himself bearing witness with our spirit that we are children of God, and if children, then heirs, heirs of God and fellow heirs with Christ, provided we suffer with him in order that we may also be glorified with him. I consider that the sufferings of this present time are not worth comparing with the glory that is to be revealed to us. For the creation waits with eager longing for the revealing of the sons of God; for the creation was subjected to futility, not of its own will but by the will of him who subjected it in hope; because the creation itself will be set free from its bondage to decay and obtain the glorious liberty of the children of God. We know that the whole creation   has been groaning in travail together until now; and not only the creation, but we ourselves, who have the first fruits of the Spirit, groan inwardly as we wait for adoption as sons, the redemption of our bodies. For in this hope we were saved. Now hope that is seen is not hope. For who hopes for what he sees? But if we hope for what we do not see, we wait for it with patience.

Likewise the Spirit helps us in our weakness; for we do not know how to pray as we ought, but the Spirit himself intercedes for us with sighs too deep for words. And he who searches the hearts of men knows what is the mind of the Spirit, because the Spirit intercedes for the saints according to the will of God. We know that in everything God works for good with those who love him, who are called according to his purpose.

For those whom he foreknew he also predestined to be conformed to the image of his Son, in order that he might be the first-born among many brethren. And those whom he predestined he also called; and those whom he called he also justified; and those whom he justified he also glorified.

What then shall we say to this? If God is for us, who is against us? He who did not spare his own Son but gave him up for us all, will he not also give us all things with him? Who shall bring any charge against God's elect? It is God who justifies; who is to condemn? Is it Christ Jesus, who died, yes, who was raised from the dead, who is at the right hand of God, who indeed intercedes for us? Who shall separate us from the love of Christ? Shall tribulation, or distress, or persecution, or famine, or nakedness, or peril, or sword? As it is written, "For thy sake we are being killed all the day long; we are regarded as sheep to be slaughtered." No, in all these things we are more than conquerors through him who loved us. For I am sure that neither death, nor life, nor angels, nor principalities, nor things present, nor things to come, nor powers, nor height, nor depth, nor anything else in all creation, will be able to separate us from the love of God in Christ Jesus our Lord. (RSV)

The next day, I took the time to listen to God. I laid aside my own agendas, and decided to let God tell me what to do. Truthfully, I don't remember what it was. But every day there were small things. One was to read my Bible. Another was to change the route I took home from work. One day I felt I needed to speak hope into my impossible situation. I typed the following declaration on a piece of paper and began to speak it every day:

> *In the Name of Jesus Christ,*
> *I place myself into the love and light of God.*
> *Thank you, God, that I will one day be in full-time ministry,*
> *teaching, preaching, and leading in worship.*
> *I speak perfect life and wholeness to my body, mind, and spirit; free*

from disease and addiction, and that I will live and not die and declare
the mighty works of the Lord.
Thank you for a wife and children.
Thank you that you will prosper the works of my hands, that I will
pay all my debts, that I will have plenty to give to the Lord and those
in need.
Thank You that I am in you, you are in me,
I am in my Father, and my Father is in me.

In November of 2004, God told me he would make a way for me to go back to Akron. At the time, I thought it was a ridiculous thought.

Over Christmas, I visited friends in Akron, and my parents in Buffalo. When my mom and Dad drove past my old apartment, my mother noticed a "for rent" sign out front.

"Maybe it's a sign from God," she said.

In January, I was making plans to return to Akron. I took a job with a national company as a full-time artist. I moved back into my old apartment building with no money down. It was pretty amazing. Of course, there were rough moments. My cash was stolen on the trip back to Ohio, and I needed the help of friends in Florida and in Ohio to make the move.

When I arrived at my apartment, my brother met me with a truckload of household items from my cousin in New York. Included among the things on the truck was a case of forty-eight rolls of toilet paper.

There were a few rough things to overcome. I had to reconcile with the pastor from St. Luke's. I had to begin to be brutally honest that I was a drug addict, and that I wasn't going to be a priest. I thought that God had brought me back to Akron to die. I had nothing to lose. Even in the midst of this, people at St. Luke's welcomed me back as a returning son. And a number of people helped me walk through the changes that needed to happen.

six: a new chapter

I LOST EVERYTHING IN FLORIDA. I really died. I died to the false self I had created, the super Christian that was a charade covering up the hurting person inside. I died to my agendas, and to my career plans. In that death, I was faced with my true self. All the ways that I had protected my image and my agenda were stripped away. I was left with nothing but a broken person, in need of God's help. As Kris Kristofferson wrote, "freedom's just another word for nothing left to lose." I was free.

Every day, I drove an hour to my job in Cleveland. During this time, I would pray. I was still committed to learning to listen to God and do what he told me. In the summer of 2005, I began to sense God calling me to pray for a house. At the time, I thought I was praying for a small house that I could use as a studio, and not need to pay rent anymore. I didn't give the matter too much thought beyond that. Around this time, I was beginning to record about an hour of worship music on tape to listen in the car. My hour commute was becoming a daily hour of prayer and worship.

In early November, I received a phone call from a friend at St. Luke's. A member of the church was taken unexpectedly to the hospital, and someone needed to stay with her son, Greg, who had advanced Parkinson's disease. I lived about a mile from Greg, so they called me to go stay with him. It was strange that they called me, since I was barely an acquaintance, but I went willingly.

Up on a hill in the west side of Akron was a 1913 Arts and Crafts house that had many unusual features. Every room on the first floor had their own exterior entrances. There was a large solarium. There were two alabaster chandeliers, and hand-made art pottery tiles around the fireplaces. It was also in gross disrepair. There was water damage on the interior walls. The plumbing was shot. There were windows missing. And there was junk everywhere. It was a mess. I put a newspaper on the couch before I sat down. As I walked around the house, I was afraid to touch anything, for fear that it would fall apart in my hands. As I walked around, I said under my breath, "God, what am I doing here?" It wasn't a prayer.

"This is the house you are praying for."

My first thought was, "Can I have another?"

This was the beginning of a new chapter in my life.

seven: pretty strange things

THE NEXT SUNDAY I VISITED A CHURCH IN CLEVELAND known for "prophetic" ministry. They had teams of people who would speak over you and pray for you. A prophetic word is simply God speaking to a person through another person. That day three ladies prayed for me. The first told me that God was about to do something really big in my life. The second lady told me to begin stocking up my cupboards with groceries. The third told me that I was about to experience a major change, and that I would not lose my apartment. Again and again, they were really excited, and said that the thing I was going to start was really big.

Needless to say, I was a little disturbed by this revelation from these well-meaning ladies. My life had just gotten settled, and I really didn't want to go through any further changes. Remember, I had given up on ministry, and was content to be a full-time artist. I had come back to Ohio to live a quiet life and then die.

But, since I received a discount on my groceries, I decided to stock my shelves with non-perishable food goods. Other than that, I was not planning on making any changes. Throughout the holidays, things were busy, and the stress at work was building. After Christmas, my job was eliminated. By January 9, I was without a job. I had one more paycheck, and Cobra insurance, so I wasn't too stressed about getting a job at first. In keeping with my new philosophy of life, I began to listen for God's direction for the next step. What I heard surprised me.

God's direction for that time was to spend time every morning at the piano in worship. In the afternoon, I was to begin writing. Nothing else. No job hunting. Fortunately, I had plenty of groceries to last me a while. In the end, the groceries lasted until June. I had also been given a twenty-four pack of toilet paper by one of my voice students. Because my company was headquartered in California, I had health insurance available to me for three years. I was holding onto the promise that I would not lose my apartment. Yet, being homeless again was a constant fear.

In late January, I was invited to a men's "encounter" retreat. I wasn't too excited, and didn't feel like bonding with other men. I was still struggling with not having a job, and I was also still using meth about once every six weeks. I was so ashamed about the drug use that I didn't tell anyone, except my doctor at the Cleveland Clinic. He was pretty persistent that I needed to quit, but I was still under the belief I could manage the problem away. On the retreat, a number of the attendees shared their personal testimonies about how God had helped them overcome a number of struggles, including drugs, sexual promiscuity, and financial failures.

On the last night of the retreat, I felt that I needed to pray with someone about the drug problem. Doing this required that I give up my artificial attitude that I was a good Christian. This was a new level of death to my own ways of solving problems. I approached a friend that I knew and trusted, and asked him to pray for me. A number of other men gathered around me, and I poured out the truth about this struggle, and how it had fed the areas of sexual weakness as well. As I "came clean" in my confession, they began to pray for me. That moment something changed. From that point on, drugs would no longer be a problem. The addictive cycle ended, and my homosexual struggle began to lessen as well. Two years later, my physician still remarks how radical the change in my life has been.

For the next three months, I continued worshiping in the morning and writing at night. I was also involved in an intensive healing program called Living Waters. For the first time, I was experiencing consistent freedom from sexual falls. My life was actually becoming more stable –even though I didn't have a "regular" job. That initial period of writing resulted in a devotional book that my church used during Lent. I was beginning to step in and be more involved in leading music for worship. Here and there, money was trickling in.

Yet, I was still concerned about not having a job. Around me there were a few people mumbling that I needed to get a job. Some of my close friends were very encouraging, but I was still uncomfortable about what was going on. At this time, being in ministry was still out of the question for me. Around this time, I began to see that I was taking the step that all artists need to take, to make the choice to live their dream, rather than talk about it. And as the old adage goes, "do what you love and the money will follow." I was learning that the only way to overcome fear is to courageously walk toward it.

The period after Easter was especially difficult. My writing project was over; my commitments for the music at church were over; and Living Waters was over. I began to pray, "God, what's next?" I continued my times of worship at the piano. I was slowly beginning to write what I would call "fragments" of songs.

In May, I received prayer from two respected members of my church. As they prayed, the wife in the couple told me that she felt the Lord saying that I needed to read the biography of George Mueller. George Mueller was a German immigrant to Great Britain who started a huge orphanage in Bristol. Mueller was unique because his ministry was funded completely by prayer. The ministry did no formal fundraising. The church that he pastored took no offerings. By the end of his life, his ministry fed and clothed over 2000 orphans. (The foundation bearing his name is still in existence.) The only request they made was that one prays for them. Mueller wanted the world to see that God still answered prayer. He claimed the promise found in Psalm 81:10: "Open your mouth wide and I will fill it."

After I finished the book, I took a few days to ponder what I had just read. Was God calling me to live by faith and prayer? By this time, I was spending several hours a day at the piano, and I was walking through my neighborhood praying for my community. One day I walked by the 1913 house and continued to pray. Across the street was a mammoth house that sat on a piece of land larger than a park. As I prayed, I sensed the Lord saying to me, "I want that house back." Now I was praying for two houses.

A few weeks later, I discovered that the big house at one time had been a Jesuit seminary.

Through this experience in the spring of 2006, I was discovering a great truth: if we still ourselves and find out what God is doing, we will discover a plan much larger than we have ever dreamed. I was beginning to see the call on my life — to be an example that God can be trusted.

Around this time, I came to an amazing conclusion: for a year and a half I had not purchased toilet paper. Ever since my move to Akron, toilet paper had been provided. First, it was the case of 48 rolls my brother brought me, then a 24 pack. After this, a friend gave me two eight packs. Then my mom bought me two four packs. Then for several weeks the rolls came one or two at a time. I was a little dumbfounded that something as humble as toilet paper was being provided, right under my nose! God was providing in an undeniable way. Over the years, I have heard it said that the devil is in the details. The truth is: God is in the details.

In late May of 2006, the Lord also began to speak to me about a coming revival. In fact, the words the Lord gave me were "You are on the cusp of the next move of God." Over the next few months, as I prayed into this, the Lord began to reveal to me that a great cataclysm was on the horizon, and that part of this was a worldwide revival. Around this time, I also felt that the Lord was directing me to begin having Holy Communion daily. This was a serious step to take, since I was not ordained in the Episcopal Church. In fact, technically you could not even assist in Holy Communion without permission. Although I had presided in Communion services prior to working in the Episcopal Church, I had not done so for twelve years. I knew that if I began to have communion without a "proper' ordination, I would one day have to leave my church. After several weeks of struggle, I decided to obey.

At the end of May, I was asked to sing at the fiftieth wedding anniversary of two friends, Vinny and Marie DeFilippo. As we planned their ceremony, we discussed all God had been doing in my life. Vinny was a gifted sculptor, and I asked him to pray for me because I was not sure what to do next. He prayed that God would make it clear if I should live by faith and work with artists.

At the anniversary party, I sat next to an old friend who was a priest. I began to tell him what was happening in my life. I began my conversation with "If you think I am off base or crazy, please tell me." I told him about the house, about not raising money, or having a regular job. I told him about the hours at the piano, and the direction God was giving me. At the end of the discussion, he looked at me with a puzzled look.

"You know, the Lord is doing some pretty strange things right now. You're not crazy."

Later, I discovered that he had just returned from the Ukraine, where some friends from our church were working as short-term missionaries. God had led them to a large house, and had directed them to not raise any money, but begin working with young people. He had heard the same story on two continents from two different people.

Things were pretty quiet in June. I was spending time with God at the piano. I was doing a few small odd jobs. Then on July 12, something happened that changed my life forever.

eight: be not afraid

THAT MORNING, A WEDNESDAY, MY PRAYER TIME was a little different. I didn't sit at the piano, but rather listened to recorded worship on a compact disc. Actually, I was dancing around my living room. As I was moving to the music, I had what I would call an "open vision." Somehow it seemed I was transported to heaven.

At first, I thought it was just my imagination, but soon I was overwhelmed by the weightiness of the atmosphere. What I saw was a place where the sky was not blue, but a luminous gold. There were mountains all around, and they too seemed to be made of a form of gold. In the center of this valley were four golden lamp stands, and around the lamps were clouds of incense. Above the lamp stands was what looked like a disc made of pure light. This light was a deep emerald green, and the edge of the disc was like the light coming from a prism forming the spectrum. As the Bible describes, there was a sea of emerald, encircled by a rainbow. The disc floated in air, and on the disc was a throne, and there was a person on the throne, but I could not see him. Actually, I don't think I could look at him. I kept looking down.

Around the pillars were four creatures, the size of elephants. They were an intense ultramarine blue. They had wings that were like eagle's wings, but they were deep red, purple, blue, and gold. The creatures were highly animated, and seemed to actually be playful, even though they were the size of monsters. Strangely, they seemed to have eyes on every side. The thing that has perplexed me the most about the vision is the depth and intensity of colors. There is no way to capture the brilliance of what I saw. I have tried with my paints and my pencils to capture it, only to give up in frustration.

I must have been standing on a high cliff above the scene because I saw a massive crowd of millions upon millions of people. From my vantage point, they were all wearing white robes. They were dancing in concentric circles around the throne, and their hands were all joined. It looked as if they were all doing the same dance, in beautiful choreography. They were filled with a rapturous joy.

As I began to take all this in, I was lifted off my feet and brought down to the farthest circle. As I approached the crowd, I saw that the people were not wearing white robes, but their own clothes. They were not doing the same dance, but each was doing their own dance. This really puzzled me, since they continued to hold hands. In the crowd, I saw faces of friends who had recently died, and even recognizable saints. They were all completely whole and alive.

At that moment, I looked up and noticed a figure approaching me. He was flying, and I assumed that he was an angel. As he got nearer, he began to communicate with me, but it was not in speech as we communicate in this world. It was almost as if it were by "telepathy." He told me to look down at the ground. Around me were bricks made of gold. The ground was paved with gold bricks.

"Do you see the ground? Do not worry about your finances. All of your financial problems, your debt, your house and everything else are worth less than one brick — even a stone from this place."

I began to be aware of my lack of faith and the fear that dictated most of my life. I began to weep.

As the angel got closer, I discovered that he was made out of what seemed to be pure fire. His face, eyes, wings, and hands were all pure fire; he was white, but it was a white fire. He was a living flame. As he approached, I began to take in the size of this being. He must have been about four meters tall. I began to bow down, and he told me to stand up.

"Stand up and do not weep, you do not know who you are." Then he reached out, touched my eyes and my ears, and I could see and hear more clearly. He put a white robe on me and touched my heart. I was given colorful wings.

The rest of the vision began to grow dim as he got closer. And he began to speak with me.

"You are called to make a way for the coming of the Lord. There are many others and I will bring them to you. You are among the firstborn among them, and you will be a father to them."

As he began to speak, the crowd began to cheer, and the living creatures flapped their wings. As they did this, one of their feathers came loose and fell.

As the vision disappeared, I realized I was standing in my living room with this angel, and there was a feather on the floor. That feather was the size of my couch! I learned very quickly that angels are sent to do a job. They are message bearers, and I had a difficult time knowing if God was speaking to me directly, or via this angel. The angel could only be described as a "pure force" sent to do a job.

The Lord continued to speak through the angel, "Things will begin to move very quickly. I will begin to bring great wealth to you. You will not ask for anything; only tell the story of what I am doing. Do not be afraid of managing great sums of wealth. I will manage it through you."

"People will bring you gifts. I am in this. Say 'yes' and receive. You will always know this is God meeting your need. Things will move very quickly, and you will know this is me."

The angel gave me his name, and told me that a great thing was about to happen. With this, the angel left. Then the vision ended.

I spent the rest of the day weeping. For several days, I told no one about what had happened. Out of the conversation with the angel, some of the pieces of the previous few months began to make sense. Over the previous year, God had brought into my life a number of incredibly gifted artists. I was beginning to see that many people really didn't believe that God answered prayer.

Throughout my experience in the church, I had seen that many people were "functional atheists." Although they said that prayer was important, and that God was alive and active, they lived their lives as though God would not act in their situations. Essentially, people are taught to work hard, make plans, and then ask God to bless those plans. It seems that it is acceptable to pray and see little or no results other than increased discipline. From the short vision I saw, the resources available to us through prayer were overwhelming.

A week later, I met with the couple who was living in the Ukraine, David and Christine Detweiler. As we began to compare notes, I was pretty astounded by the vision God had given them to create a house for young creative people. I was impressed that God had given them a similar direction, to not do traditional fundraising, and to pray for their income.

I have to say that this was not an easy move to make. I was struggling about having a regular job. Every time I did attempt to find work, everything seemed to stop. I finally began to remind myself of Father Al's advice:

Listen to the Lord, and do what he tells you.

THE GLORY OF A WASTED LIFE

nine: you are not alone

SEVERAL THINGS DEVELOPED DURING THAT SUMMER. I was teaching voice lessons to a number of people. God was beginning to make the needs of creative people more clear to me. My lessons began to be more focused on working through the roadblocks that prevent entering the creative life that God had called my students. There seemed to be a layer of fear that hung over all of these gifted men and women. When I compared my story to theirs, it seemed that all the power of hell and humanity warred against artists. No one wanted them to walk into their destiny.

During the time after the angelic encounter, I was learning some new lessons in prayer. There seemed to be a new authority, and a new level of influence that accompanied my prayers. After seeing heaven, and seeing how the angel responded to me, I was beginning to understand the authority God has given us. If we are seated with Christ, as the New Testament says, then demons who are far below fallen humanity have no power over us. If we are seated with Christ in heavenly places, then disease and sickness should not have power over us. At the time, I kept these epiphanies to myself. Most of all, I was beginning to understand the vocation on my life.

Slowly, financial gifts to the "ministry" were beginning to flow in. Amazingly, my landlord let me continue to live in my apartment, even though I was several months behind in my rent. This was astounding. God was confronting my fear, and keeping his promise: I would not lose my apartment.

In early August, it was becoming clear that I would need to leave St. Luke's and eventually I would separate myself from the Anglican Church. For thirteen years, clergy had questioned my call, and said I was not fit for ministry. At the same time, they were quick to let me work for free. This "crazy making" did more than anything else to fuel my struggle with homosexuality. At the same time, the Episcopal Church and the worldwide Anglican Communion were splintering apart over homosexuality. My choice to walk into radical obedience was changing my attitude toward the church, and making me less willing to submit to its authority.

On August 12, my birthday, I went on a drive with my friend Kevin into the country. In Massillon, Ohio, we noticed a big church on a hill. We decided to go look at it, and Kevin wondered if it would be unlocked.

"It will be open for me," I joked.

When we approached the church doors, we discovered that someone had propped the church doors open. Upon entering the church, we were both stunned by the beauty, size, and design of the windows. Immediately, I was overwhelmed by the strong presence of the Holy Spirit in the church. I decided to go up to the altar to pray. When I looked up at the tabernacle on the altar, where the consecrated bread was kept, the doors were open and the silk curtains were pulled back. Normally, the curtain would be pulled closed, and the doors would be locked. I knew this was very strange, and I began to pray.

At that moment, I was overwhelmed with an awareness of the Glory of God, and it was like a golden fog. As the weight of the glory overwhelmed me, my eyes were opened, and I saw the angel who had visited me in July. He flew down from the altar and approached me. What happened to me next both shocked and amazed me.

A female figure, about five feet tall, approached me. She reminded me of Mother Theresa, and how she walked with humility, but also with great dignity. She knelt on the rail next to me, and put her arm around my shoulder.

The angel began to communicate with me, much as before.

"You have been faithful and God is pleased with you. Do not be afraid, and stay the course. Gifts will begin today, and they will not cease. I will provide for all of your needs. Do not be afraid, for you are not alone."

By this point, I was sobbing. The woman was embracing me, and Jesus was there in front of both of us. The angel continued to communicate as God's messenger. He began to speak to us:

"You have gone through a very difficult time, you have been faithful, and I have been with you. This new work is being birthed through you. This is your labor.

"I want my mother involved in this work. All creativity is near to her heart. She has made answer for all creation, and I want her involved in this new work.

"Do not be afraid; stay the course."

I was sobbing pretty hard, and Kevin ran to find some Kleenex. Much like the earlier experience, I was overwhelmed, speechless. I was overcome by my own lack of faith, and my heart despaired.

I prayed and told Jesus that I would do whatever he asked.

By that time, I guess about half an hour, I had heard and seen all that I could bear. Between the visions and the weeping, I was feeling exhausted. I prayed a brief prayer and told Kevin that I needed to go.

That day I was pretty quiet, and wept here and there.

There was a lot that happened in the church that I did not understand. God was calling me to a work of creation. More specifically, a work of Incarnation: putting flesh on his Presence. More and more I was learning the meaning of the words "with God all things are possible."

Oh Lord, I am your servant.
I am your servant, and the child of your handmaiden.
You have freed me from my bonds. (Psalm 116:14)

THE GLORY OF A WASTED LIFE

ten: favor

THE NEXT DAY, I ATTENDED METRO CHURCH, the church in Cleveland where the women had prophesied over me the previous year. To my surprise, there was a guest speaker that day. Marc Dupont was a pastor in Dayton, Ohio. I had crossed paths with Marc several times before, and each time, it was a significant event in my life. It seemed that whenever I encountered his ministry, God started something new in my life.

During the sermon, Marc seemed to confirm a lot that God had been doing in the previous weeks. At the end of the sermon, he asked if there was anyone there who was in need of healing. At the time, my HIV status was still not good. I was on some medication that was making me sick most of the time, and my viral load was pretty bad. But I was not eager to go forward for prayer, mostly because I didn't want someone to ask me why I needed prayer, and have to go through the awkwardness of their shock.

Unfortunately, in the Christian community, there is very little understanding about being HIV positive and having AIDS, just as there is little nuance between struggling with a homosexual orientation and espousing a "gay" lifestyle.

Just as I was about to forgo receiving prayer, Marc Dupont continued:

"If there is anyone here from Roger and Gretsie's church, St. Luke's, we would like you to stand up."

I stood up, and looked around. There was no one else. Marc pointed at me and said, "Come forward, we want to pray for you." It is not often that I have been summoned to the front for prayer in a church service, no less one where I was visiting. As I went forward, I had a sense of expectation that something was about to happen. As I stood there, Marc came up behind me and said, "Lord, cleanse this man's blood." Then some others gathered around me to pray. At that moment, I felt something happen.

It turns out that there was supposed to be a group from the St. Luke's ministry team there that Sunday. None of them showed up, and I was the only person from St. Luke's there.

That week I went to Cleveland and had my blood tested. At seven o'clock Friday night, my doctor called me and told me that my viral load was undetectable. I shared this in church on Sunday, and eight confirmed healings occurred. My life was taking an interesting turn. Another wave of healing would flow through the church when those who had been healed shared their testimonies.

By this time, I would get up every morning, and ask God, "What's on the agenda?"

Around this time, I heard the Lord tell me to find twelve people to pray for me regularly. Of course, the recent events had gotten a lot of people's attention. It was fairly easy to get that first group of twelve. In the next few weeks, I began sending emails to my "prayer team," to make them aware of critical prayer needs. By mid-fall, I was sending out one email a week, now and again, two. Eventually, I had forty people on the list. By winter, the emails had taken on a "life of their own." God was creating a cyber community that was growing steadily. It was exciting to see people commit to pray daily for me, and the few friends that were beginning to gather with me.

Again and again, we continued to pray for the house. The folks on the email list would send me things God was showing them in prayer. Repeatedly, I would receive emails telling me that God wanted to make the house an "embassy of heaven."

During this time, I was beginning to experience several new things. First, what I had described as "fragments" of songs were beginning to take on the shape of full songs. Although they were short, they were could really be called songs. At this time, I was also beginning to have an experience during my daily Bible study that was really new. Insight and understanding of the Bible were opening up to me like never before. The "dots" that I had seen all along were beginning to come together. For example, here is a journal entry from 21 August 2006:

Sin has consequences. They are serious, and they can be destructive, but they are limited. Because sin is not creative, the effects of sin are not limitless. At some point, sin's effects will run out.

By contrast, the effects of obedience and faithfulness to God, because they are part of the creative life of God, are limitless. When we obey God, this obedience multiplies and replicates, much in the way cells multiply and replicate. As it says in the scripture:

". . . for I the LORD your God am a jealous God, visiting the iniquity of the fathers upon the children to the third and fourth generation of those who hate me, but showing steadfast love to thousands of those who love me and keep my commandments." (Deuteronomy 5:9-10)

This is good news.

More and more, as I prayed in the neighborhood, and in my private times of prayer, I would return to the sixty-first and sixty-second chapters of the prophet Isaiah:

> The Spirit of the Lord God is upon me,
> Because the Lord has anointed me
> to bring good tidings to the afflicted,
> he has sent me to bind up the broken hearted,
> To proclaim liberty to the captives,
> and the opening of the prison to those who are bound;
> To proclaim the year of the Lord's favor,
> and the day of vengeance for our God;
> To comfort all who mourn;
> To grant to those who mourn in Zion —
> to give them a garland instead of ashes,
> The oil of gladness instead of mourning,
> the mantle of praise instead of a faint spirit;
> That they may be called oaks of righteousness,
> the planting of the Lord, that he might be glorified.
> They shall build up the ancient ruins,
> They shall raise up the former devastations;
> They shall repair the ruined cities,
> The devastations of many generations.
> Aliens shall stand and feed your flocks,
> Foreigners shall be your plowmen and vinedressers;
> But you shall be called priests of the Lord,
> Men shall speak of you as ministers of our God;
> You shall meet the wealth of nations,
> And in their riches you shall glory.
> Instead of shame you shall have a double portion,
> Instead of dishonor you shall rejoice in your lot;
> Therefore, in your land you shall receive a double portion;
> Yours shall be everlasting joy.
> For I the Lord love justice,

I hate robbery and wrong;
I will faithfully give them their recompense,
And I will make an everlasting covenant with them.
Their descendants shall be known among the nations,
And their offspring in the midst of the peoples;
All who see them shall acknowledge them,
That they are people the Lord has blessed.
I will greatly rejoice in the Lord,
My soul shall exult in my God;
For he has clothed me with the garments of salvation,
He has covered me with the robe of righteousness,
As bridegroom decks himself with a garland,
And as a bride adorns herself with her jewels.
For as the earth brings forth its shoots,
And as a garden causes what is sown in it to spring up,
So the Lord will cause righteousness
and praise to spring forth for all the nations.
For Zion's sake I will not keep silent,
And for Jerusalem's sake I will not rest,
Until her vindication goes forth as brightness,
And her salvation as a burning torch.
The nations shall see your vindication,
And all the kings your glory
And you shall be called by a new name
which the mouth of the Lord will give.
You shall be a crown of beauty in the hand of the Lord,
and a royal diadem in the hand of our God.
You shall no longer be termed Forsaken,
and your land shall no longer be called Desolate;
But you will be called My Delight is in Her, and your land Married;
For the Lord delights in you, and your land shall be married.
For as a young man marries a virgin, so shall your sons marry you,
and as the bridegroom rejoices over the bride,
so shall your God rejoice over you.
Upon your walls, O Jerusalem,
I have set watchmen,
All the day and all the night

They shall never be silent.
You who put the Lord in remembrance,
Take no rest
And give him no rest until he establishes Jerusalem
and makes it a praise in the earth.
The Lord has sworn by his right hand and by his mighty arm:
"I will not again give your grain to be food for your enemies,
and foreigners shall not drink your wine
for which you have labored;
But those who garner it shall eat it and praise the Lord,
And those who gather it shall drink it in the courts of my sanctuary."
Go through, Go through the gates, prepare the way for the people:
Build up, build up the highway, make it clear of stones,
lift up an ensign for the peoples.
Behold, the Lord has proclaimed to the end of the earth:
Say to the daughter of Zion,
"Behold your salvation comes; behold,
his reward is with him, and his recompense is before him."
And they shall be called the Holy People,
The redeemed of the Lord;
And you shall be called Sought out,
A city not forsaken.

THE GLORY OF A WASTED LIFE

eleven: a blank check

ON SEPTEMBER 8, I ATTENDED A CONFERENCE at Metro Church. The conference itself was not that exciting, but during the break, I began to ponder some of the things that I had been reading. One of these things was a term that George Muller had referred to repeatedly in his writing and in his journals. When asked where he kept his money and resources, he referred to the "Bank that would not break."

During this break, I began to pray and ask God if this bank was a real place, or simply a metaphor that Muller used. As I was praying, I began to see an image of a large bank. As before, everything in the bank was made of gold. As I looked around, I saw a man behind the counter, and approached the teller. Unlike a normal bank, behind the teller were large piles of gold, precious stones, and various kinds of material riches. I asked him what all of this was. He told me, "These are the riches you have laid up in heaven."

At that moment, I saw in my hands a blank check.

"Go ahead, write a check," a voice said.

I was afraid because I didn't want to spend my inheritance.

"This is not your inheritance," the voice said. "This is only the treasure you have laid up in heaven, go ahead and write a check."

I began to write my check. I decided that $1 million was as ludicrous an amount as I could accept. I sensed the Lord stopping me.

"That is not a very big check here. Why don't you write it for the wealth of nations?"

With that, I did.

The teller looked at me, smiled and told me that large checks are delivered in $1 million increments. Then I saw a large briefcase filled with cash. The teller handed it to me.

With that, the vision ended.

When we worship, we have power and influence in heaven. We have the power and authority to move things seen and unseen. I was beginning to develop a sense of expectation that the things I have prayed for would begin to happen, one by one. I grew bolder in prayer. I began to expect opportunities.

Again, I was learning to overcome fear.

twelve: tangible results

THROUGHOUT THE PREVIOUS MONTHS, I BEGAN "PRAYER WALKING" the neighborhood more diligently. Prayer walking is a way to intercede for your community while walking through the neighborhood. I often repeat scripture verses on a small rosary. In the evenings, I usually walked through the streets near my apartment. I paid close attention to evidence of criminal activity, spiritual activity like occultism, or occult graffiti, and the "vibe" in the neighborhood. Before long, I began to make my routine three points. These points made a triangle in my neighborhood. The three points were a dance studio that also was involved in Reiki, a form of spiritual healing; a psychic studio, and a church in my neighborhood.

After several months of praying through the neighborhood, God began to show me how to pray for these three points. This was a time when I was also beginning to grow in my sense of authority in prayer. God began moving me to pray that I would be invited to lead worship in the church. God showed me that I should pray that crime would cease in the neighborhood. One night, when I was walking by the psychic studio, I sensed that God was telling me to take authority over the demonic power that was strengthening the person who owned the studio. I pointed at the building, and prayed:

"In Jesus' name, as the authority in this neighborhood, I declare that all demonic power in this business must go and never come back. This neighborhood will be a place where life and light reign."

I went on my way that night, and really didn't expect much more activity. A week later, I was riding the bus, and looked up and saw that the psychic studio was closed. About two weeks later, the sign was gone, the windows were dark, and a "for rent" sign was up. That was a little frightening. Over the next few months, I began to step out into prayer in a few new ways, and several of my friends joined me.

One of these locations was the Union Gospel Press building in Tremont, an old neighborhood in Cleveland. The building had a reputation for ghosts, and was on several of the "Cleveland's Most Haunted Places" lists. On September 26, 2006, I took my friend Kevin to the building. We had Holy Communion there, and felt that God was telling us to break a stronghold of bitterness over the property. The place was incredibly creepy. We stood on the stoop, and held the bread inside the big iron gates. Then we broke the bread, sprinkled a little holy water, and left.

Nothing dramatic happened, but we felt a lightness in the atmosphere. Afterward, we met some friends for dinner, and I felt the Lord nudging me to go back to Tremont.

We had noticed a circle of stones in a patch of grass in the neighborhood near the Gospel Press building. In the center of the circle was a small apple tree. I didn't know what that space was used for, but had a hunch that it was a place of spiritual activity.

After dinner, in the dark, we quietly went to the circle. I had saved some of the consecrated bread from the earlier prayer time, and we stepped into the circle. I did nothing other than break the bread, and then we prayed the Lord's Prayer. Suddenly, a real sense of freedom broke out over me, and I began to praise and thank God. My friends were eager to leave, so we did.

In the car on the way home, I began to feel sick. It reminded me of the time I got a bad electrical shock that made me feel queasy and a little disoriented. Beyond that, I didn't know what had happened.

That night, I had a dream. In the dream I saw three angels, who were all very tall. They looked like Roman soldiers, and they had shields and broad swords. They stood in the circle of stones in Tremont. As they stood there, they thrust their swords into the ground, and stood in three directions. One faced southwest, one faced northwest, and one faced northeast. As they stood there, a group of angels began to descend and fly through the three angels. As they did this, they formed what looked like a "highway." The highway began to become a passage for the angels to enter Tremont. Then I saw an angel stand at the front of the roof of each house in the neighborhood, with a sword drawn, as if he were standing guard.

The next morning I began sharing the details of this dream with my friend Kevin and remarked how I thought it was strange that there were three angels. Truthfully, I thought it was a fanciful dream, and expected that if there were going to be angels, there should be four.

Kevin looked at me and said, "Of course there were three, there were three 'lay' lines there."

I was stunned.

I had never heard of lay lines before. After some questions, Kevin explained to me that the spot we had ventured onto the previous night was a "node." Nodes are places where electromagnetic fields in the earth's crust meet, and these places are used for occult activity. I didn't really understand this, and was actually pretty skeptical, so I went to the library to do some research. What I discovered was surprising.

Not only did I find a number of references to "lay" lines, I learned that the early Christian missionaries to Europe understood their power. When looking at aerial photographs of Great Britain, one can clearly see that churches and shrines were built in line with one another. Throughout Europe, cathedrals were often placed where these lines intercepted. Although the missionaries were often building on top of pagan worship sites, the sites were built along these ancient lines.

Then I looked at the map of Cleveland, and discovered our circle had been constructed in the geographic center of Cleveland, on a small triangle of land. When I drew lines out from the circle in the direction of the angels in my dream, I discovered that lines went through three distinct areas of Cleveland. In each case, the neighborhoods along the line were pockets of extreme poverty, one of them being East Cleveland, the poorest city in the country. One line went to Akron, one went to Buffalo, and the third went to Toledo. I was beginning to feel a little like a conspiracy theorist.

I also did some research about the Gospel Press Building. The property had once been a Christian publishing house. In the 1990's some artists had obtained it and tried to form an arts community there, only to have a number of disagreements and finally disband. I was unaware of this history when we went to pray the previous night.

Several weeks later, I drove through the neighborhood to see if anything had changed. There were a number of improvement projects underway. The streets were being repaved, a number of new buildings were being built, and they were beginning to renovate the Gospel Press Building. I also learned that a number of abandoned buildings in East Cleveland were being renovated, and have since been occupied. My understanding of prayer was beginning to change. There seemed to be tangible results to the prayers we had prayed weeks earlier.

THE GLORY OF A WASTED LIFE

thirteen: only a few things

THE NEXT SEVERAL MONTHS (ACTUALLY UNTIL THE FOLLOWING MAY), I began to get off track. This happens to many ministries. I got really excited about new things happening, and especially that fall, I began to attract a number of new people into my life who were excited about the work I was doing. I was really insecure as well. As the year ended, I began to transition out of the Anglican Church. By Christmas, I was finished after fourteen years.

A number of the people around me were giving me suggestions about how I should manage my time, manage the ministry, how I should promote things. We had a number of public meetings. We had meetings on Sunday nights. A friend moved into the apartment next to mine, and we began sharing meals and meeting for prayer daily. I began to "build the ministry" just like the church plant in Kentucky, and the businesses I had been involved in. I also took advice from people about my health, and stopped taking my HIV medication.

At the same time, I was still attempting to listen to God as best I could. When I took the time to listen to God, and paid attention to pleasing Him, God had success. One of these great successes was spending time in a local coffee shop.

The Nervous Dog Coffee Bar had recently opened in the fall of 2006. God began directing me to hang out there on a regular basis. Eventually, the Lord provided a new laptop, and I was spending my time there writing. By the spring, I had begun to develop relationships with key leaders in my community.

Unfortunately, I was spending more time trying to "do the right thing" and please those around me. I also had a deep need to be busy, so I started doing all kinds of things to "network." I signed up for non-profit business classes. I taped signs all over the city. I coerced a friend to give the ministry money for advertising. My relationship with my friend, who had moved in, ended badly.

Worst of all, the decision to stop using my medication caused a relapse of my health. By June, I felt like a real failure. I began to ask God where I had gotten off track. Throughout the summer, God began to show me the areas where I had tried to make the ministry happen, rather than do what he had called me to do. When I began to look over my journal, there were only a few things the Lord had clearly directed: to raise up an army of artists, to pray and worship, and to hang out at the coffee shop. When I did those things, God blessed me.

In January, I went with some friends to the International House of Prayer in Kansas City, Missouri. Since 1999, the IHOP, as it is called, has had an ongoing prayer and worship meeting happening around the clock. While there, I was impressed that I needed to pray in downtown Akron. There was an old school building that had recently been renovated by Akron Pregnancy Services, our local crisis pregnancy center. God told me to ask if I could begin praying there daily. When I came home, I met with the director, and she was excited. By the afternoon of our meeting, I had a set of keys to the school. They had given it the name "NOIZ."

These times at Noiz brought a transformation and focus to my prayer time I had not known before. I was beginning to write extended songs.

Every day, I went and began to pray at Noiz. In the afternoon, I went to the coffee shop.

By the spring, I was meeting all of the local pastors. As I mentioned earlier, two years before I would "prayer walk" my neighborhood! One of the points on my walk was the Fairlawn West United Church of Christ, one block from my house. The pastor hung out at the coffee shop, and one day we began to have a conversation. At the end of the chat, he offered me the use of his building. We began meeting in the church on Sunday nights. It would be several months before I realized this was an answer to my prayer two years earlier.

During this period, I also began to discover that many others in Akron had been praying for the house on the hill. In fact, there were people who had been praying for nine years that the house would be used for ministry. I also began to meet men and women who had been called to Akron to pray, some for as long as twenty years. I was beginning to wonder what God was doing.

fourteen: another shot

MY HEALTH WAS NOT GREAT THROUGHOUT THE EARLY PART OF 2007. I was second-guessing a lot of my decisions, and I was wondering if I had made too many wrong turns. I wondered if I should quit this crazy life, and go find a regular job. My friend Carrie was a huge encouragement at the time, and she often would give me a "pep talk."

"If you don't step out and continue this, who will?" She would ask. She would rattle back to me things that I had said a year before, such as "Remember, God can be trusted."

Then a real surprise came in early August. Marc Dupont sent me an email.

Christ,
as much as you must be discouraged at the return of the symptoms, I want
to encourage you to really press into the Lord for the complete
healing. I don't know why the symptoms have returned, but I do know that
the good works that God begins He is faithful to complete.

We are having a strong emphasis on healing at our annual Mantle of
Praise conference. It is the 28th - 30th of this month. On the Friday, from
9.30am to 3.30 p.m. we are having a stand-alone healing seminar with Ian
Andrews and myself. I would like to invite you as my guest to the day
seminar. We, Ian, myself, and my ministry team would pray for you at least
a couple of times throughout the day when we have ministry times. You
can go to the following web site: www.daytonvineyard.com for information
on the focus and speakers, etc.

I know God did something significant with you when we prayed for
you last summer. Possibly, like the blind man Jesus prayed for who was
only partially healed until Jesus prayed for him again, there is another
significant touch of the Holy Spirit needed. I am believing God to do that.

Please let me know if you can attend and I will make sure your name tags and registration for the day are taken care of.

Yours in prayer,

Marc A. Dupont

"The knowledge of the Glory of God will cover the earth, as the waters cover the seas"!

I was astonished. At the end of September, Carrie and I decided to drive to Dayton, and went to the conference. I wasn't sure what might happen, but I was willing to give it another shot.

Early in the morning of September 28, we got in the car and began the three-hour trip to Dayton. We got there in time for the conference to begin, and sat a few rows from the front. During the first session, Ian Andrews, who I had never heard of before, gave a short instructional teaching on praying for the sick. Then he called someone from the audience up on the platform and asked them to try it. A shy young woman came forward and joined Ian. Nervously, the woman spoke into the microphone, pointed in my direction and said: "In the name of Jesus Christ, be healed."

As she spoke, I felt something happen, like a layer of dirt came off my body. I looked over at Carrie. She was staring at me.

"What are you looking at?" I asked.

"You are a different color," she said.

For the rest of the day, she kept staring at me. Marc and Ian prayed for me again before we drove home. Although they invited people to testify if they thought they were healed, I was not too eager to stand up and say I was healed. After the previous experience, I was very cautious.

After two days, I admitted something had happened. All of the side effects from my medication had stopped. My energy levels were very high, and as I mentioned, my complexion had become pretty rosy. Even with this, I waited to have my blood work taken for another two months at my regular doctor's appointment. At the end of November, I received an email from my physician.

Once again, my viral load was undetectable.

fifteen: an ongoing parable

TODAY, MY LIFE HAS BEEN NARROWED DOWN to the essential things that God has directed me to do. I wake up in the morning and begin the day reading the scripture. I pray and then have Holy Communion. I spend a couple hours at the Nervous Dog, and my afternoons in prayer and worship at NOIZ. I have given up "networking." Sounds like a recipe for failure to most people.

Actually, my phone rings pretty often with people wanting to talk to me. Men and women, who are spiritually hungry, approach me in the coffee, and ask if I will talk with them or pray for them. There are over 100 people who have signed up for the email list, and these folks ask for prayer as well. Every day I have a "divine appointment" with someone who is either in need of encouragement, or someone that I need to know. Things are always expanding.

The prayer time at NOIZ is now beginning to attract others who are interested in praying there. I am approached regularly about beginning a place of ongoing prayer and worship. Artists who are hungry to use their gifts have begun to come to me, rather than me trying hard to attract them.

I continue to do no fundraising, and only publicize needs to those who pray for me. The bills get paid, and as we expand, those needs are being covered as well. I only tell the story of what God is doing in my life, and he supplies my needs. I have two full years behind me, and have come to believe that God is faithful, and that God can be trusted. There is nothing to fear.

In December of 2007, I began to sense the Lord telling me that we would be in the house by Christmas. The woman who owned the property died the week after Thanksgiving. As I prayed, I thought about the impossible, and how that would be pretty impossible. As the month went on, I continued to ask the Lord what that might mean. As Christmas approached, my stress level continued to rise. Christmas Eve came and still nothing happened.

In the afternoon on December 24, a friend of mine invited me to join him at Midnight Mass. He told me a number of his friends got together every Christmas and attended Midnight Mass. As we talked, I learned that most of them had grown up in Christian homes, but they were tired of the hypocrisy. These "twenty-somethings" all wanted integrity in their own lives, in the face of the struggles they each had with drugs, with finding a purpose in life, and with having an authentic relationship with God.

In the snow we stood outside St. Bernard's while most of the groups had a cigarette. There was a little bit of snow coming down. I discovered that I was invited into a group that had been meeting at Christmas for several years. As we went into church, and the music began, I heard the Lord speak. "This is the house you are building, Christ."

I am still praying for the house on the hill, but now see it as a piece of the larger fabric of my life. I have now committed sixteen hours a week to prayer and worship. Others have begun to join me. This parable continues to be written, and toilet paper continues to roll in.

sixteen: God is good

SO AS I MENTIONED IN THE BEGINNING OF THIS BOOK, I believe that God is raising up an army. As Henri Nouwen said, these are men and women who are "wounded healers." I guess the point is, if you are willing to get up, confess your sin, and turn from your wicked ways, you are not disqualified from the new thing that God is doing. In fact, you may be the most qualified.

For the past century, the church in the West has been built on the idea that only the best-looking, best-educated, and most "squeaky clean" can be in ministry. In the end, we have ended up with a church that appears very successful on the outside, but is really a shell of shallow people who are not being honest about their struggles and their sin. In the face of real challenges, this form of godliness with no power has been just that: powerless. As a result, the sheep have left the flock in droves, willing to risk facing the wolves themselves, rather than being under the care of hired servants. I often talk to men and women who are fine to dabble in the occult or non-Christian spirituality because they have discovered power.

As you have seen from my story, I tried to be one of those outwardly strong types. God, in his mercy, gave me a problem that was bigger than I was. I have to face this struggle every day and cry out for mercy and for help. As Mother Theresa prayed, "Jesus, stay close by me today, or I will betray you like Judas." This is the beginning of wisdom.

Why is God raising up a bunch of screwed up people?

Because we are the ones who know we are poor. God is looking for those who will go after his riches. Anything else is not the Kingdom. You see, God is the king of the Kingdom. Anything else, whether it is a spiritual movement, a denomination, a church office, a government, or any human structure, is less than the kingdom. God has allowed these structures to exist until the time would come when the King could come and restore the Kingdom. I believe that the time of restoration is approaching.

We are no longer headed toward a time when "survival of the fittest" will be our philosophy. Now is the time of the "thriving of the weakest."

> For consider your call brothers and sisters; not many of you were wise according to worldly standards, not many were powerful, not many were of noble birth; but God chose what is foolish in the world to shame the wise, God chose what is weak in the world to shame the strong, God chose what is low and despised in the world, even things that are not, to bring to nothing, things that are, so that no human being might boast in the presence of God." (I Corinthians 1:26-29)

God has been shaking things for a while. Last year, both of my grandmothers died in their eighties. They both asked me before their death if I knew what was happening in the world. They knew that something was in the air. Things are shaking.

I was part of one of the largest denominational structures in the world. For nearly 500 years, the Anglican Church has managed to weather a number of problems and continue to expand worldwide. Over the span of ten years, that worldwide structure has not only been shaken, it seems to be disintegrating. Other denominations are experiencing this same phenomena. Church as usual is ceasing to exist. Jesus is the King of the Kingdom.

Last year, the largest church in the United States admitted that they were unsuccessful at making disciples. Several folks sent me emails saying they had "repented" of their methods. When I watched the video presentation on the Internet, I saw that there was little repentance. What I saw was another version of "try harder." Their attitude was we need to find another method, since the current one was not working. I am afraid that they will continue to have failure. Jesus is the King of the Kingdom, and any other method outside of Kingdom will fail.

So what is kingdom? Kingdom is slow, and it is messy. Kingdom demands getting on your face before God every morning and asking "What is on the agenda today?" I have to do this, because I have learned that I really don't know what is on God's agenda. More and more, God is directing the agenda. There have been many days when I have just sat in silence, as much as I felt the need to cry out. I have given up the schedule and the promotional activity.

I have even given up networking. God chooses the perfect death for each of us. For me, it is building something in my own strength. His strength is perfect in my weakness. So I choose weakness.

Kingdom is being willing to sit alone on a Sunday night and be faithful in prayer and worship, even if your big crowd doesn't show up. Kingdom is being willing to not do a bunch of manipulative fundraising schemes, and believing that if God said he would provide, God will provide. Kingdom is laying aside your manual, your schedule, your palm-pilot, and your method for the guidance of the One who has the most at stake. It means listening and not running ahead – not doing anything if God doesn't give you direction. And it means obedience if God does.

The hardest lesson I have learned in the past three years is to not pursue something if God doesn't direct it. I have failed to draw a crowd many times. My success is not based on the size of the crowd — that is human insecurity. God does not reward success; God rewards faithfulness. And in the end, I want to be found faithful. I want to look in his eyes and hear the words "Well done, you good and faithful servant."

So where is God moving? God is moving toward creating a place where he feels comfortable living. God is looking for a place where there are worshippers, worshiping in spirit and in truth. He is looking for a place where he can inhabit. God is looking for a place where his Glory may abide, where his Son can have a Bride, and where there is unbroken fellowship and communion with his people. We will be his people, and He will be our God.

And who is he recruiting to create this place? He is looking for the broken, the hurting, the needy, and the helpless to build this place. You see, they are the only ones who he can trust. The strong and the smart have been at it for about 1800 years, and they have spilled a lot of blood, and they have built a lot of big buildings. Unfortunately, they have also not asked God about his methods. The end does not justify the means in the Kingdom. The strong will say "we have done all these great things in your name. We have a 4.5 acre parking lot and a jumbotron and five services on a weekend, and we have built hospitals and opened social service agencies and had voter registration drives, and we have handed out tracts, and have family nights at church." And the master of the house will say, "Depart from me, I never knew you."

I am still praying for a house and the properties in my city. There are days that I wonder if I should keep it up. I often wonder if I will look like a fool in the end. I have come to realize that the point isn't about a building or a budget, or even if there is large group of artists all worshiping night and day (although, I would love to see all of that).

The point is developing a relationship with God. I know that at the end of the day, when the master comes, he will know me. If nothing else, this was worth it, to know him. If I am misunderstood, if I am made a fool, at least I know him. When I see him, I won't be meeting a stranger, I will be reunited with a friend, and there will be nothing separating us. That's the glory of a wasted life, to know him, to love him, and to be in his presence. And when you do that, you become like him. He doesn't want a big building with his name on it; he wants a bunch of people filled with his DNA. He wants you to look like your Father in heaven. He wants you to do the things you see your Father doing. He wants you seated at his right hand. Anything else is not the Kingdom. Anything else is not God.

That's a pretty radical proposition. We serve a pretty radical God. The most powerful man in the universe is doing something radical. Jesus is before the Father, interceding. He's praying. That's what he does. If it's good enough for Jesus, then it's good enough for me. Why is he praying? So that the Kingdom will come, and that it will be on earth as it is in heaven. So that we will be his people, and He will be our God.

There is coming a day when his house will be a house of prayer. Jerusalem will be a praise in the earth. People from every tongue and tribe and nation will gather and worship before him. These weak and broken people will bring the best they have to him. There will be art and music, fine robes and dancing. The finest things ever made will be brought before him, as offerings to a King. We will kneel before him, at the name of Jesus, and he will reign. There will be no sickness, there will be no sin, and there will be no death. We will not need the light of the sun or the moon by night because He will be our light. We will share in the glory of everything as it should be. It will be better than it was originally intended.

This is the highest call we human beings can have, to minister to God, to pray, and to seek the Kingdom. From a worldly standard, it is a complete waste. I invite you to join me in building a place for God. Let God show you the path you need to take. There is no sin so great that will keep you from joining in the plan of God. You haven't missed the path, or made too many wrong turns. God will give you the key to unlock the puzzles in your life if you will only let him. It is scary, and it might feel like a big jump, but you can learn to trust him.

God is good, and he can be trusted.

Listen, and do what he tells you.

afterword: some practical advice

AGAIN AND AGAIN IN MY CHRISTIAN EXPERIENCE, I have encountered men and women who choose to enter into "survival mode." Survival mode is an attitude a person adopts where they become fixated on meeting a need or set of needs. We all have needs, and many of those needs are healthy, normal, and good. Yet, we were not made to meet our needs. When we become consumed with meeting a need, we will soon begin to miss the rich, abundant life God has for us, and we cease to thrive.

We were not created to meet our own needs. This is especially evident with the needs to be nurtured, loved, and accepted. At the very least, these needs are to be met first by our parents, then by significant people in our lives. Ultimately, our needs must be met in God. They must be met through developing an intimate relationship with the One who knows us best. When we know God, we can begin to know ourselves, and to become known by others. To seek to meet our deep needs through sex, career, relationships, objects, and success short-circuits the process of becoming whole. We become diminished persons. This striving to survive moves from being at the very least sinful human effort to a truly satanic manifestation that creates chaos in every direction.

When Jesus said, "seek first the kingdom, and its righteousness, and all these things shall be added to you," he was talking about the survival mode. The gospel invites us to set aside the struggle to survive. We are called to step out of the "food chain" and into a relationship with the Holy Spirit. In coming into contact with God, we are confronted with our inadequacies and forced to rely on God's help. We can't meet our needs. We can't make our success happen we can't become whole persons. We can't thrive on our owne. We can't "pull ourselves up by our bootstraps and try harder." We aren't equipped with straps strong enough. Most of us don't even have any boots. We are in desperate need. Our only hope is to seek God first.

Something extraordinary happens when we surrender to God and give up trying to meet our own needs. The cycle of survival begins to unwind. We are no longer trying to get ahead. We come to the same place Lily Tomlin did when she said, "Even if you win the rat race, you are still a rat." Instead, you are free to actually do good things. You don't have to be consumed with "what do I get out of this?" You can begin to give to others. You can give up your seat on the bus. You can begin to live selflessly.

The best advice I can give someone in a real struggle to survive is to find a place where you can volunteer and give to others. One Christmas, when I had no money and was on the verge of losing my apartment, I volunteered for an organization that gave toys to needy families. I took the focus off myself and put it on others. Two things happened. First, I assumed a place of abundance, even though I actually had very little. Secondly, I actually forgot about my survival mode for a while. I experienced real joy. That is the first step toward thriving. There is no situation or pain so great that you can seek to live out the kingdom and put someone else first. You will discover yourself becoming more human and less beastly.

When you let God meet your needs, you get a great surprise. God meets your need, and then gives you more than you even wanted. God's nature is to be generous, good, and abundant. If you make the sacrifice to give up your agenda, God will take what you have surrendered and return it to you beyond your expectations. I see this again and again, in finances, relationships, and resources. Generosity overflows and returns to you. God's plan for us is to thrive: to be full of joy, peace, patience, goodness, gentleness, kindness, and self-control. When you begin to live out of that abundant place, the world will begin to knock on your door. Then you are the richest person in the neighborhood.

There are a few practical steps to living a life surrendered to God. First, you have to begin a relationship with Jesus Christ. The easiest way to do this is to find a quiet place and pray this simple prayer:

God, I want to know you. The only way I can know you is to know Jesus Christ. I believe that Jesus died on the cross for me, and that he rose again from the dead. I want him to be Lord in my life. I confess my sin to you (take a moment and confess any specific sin that comes to your mind). I thank you for forgiving my sin, giving me the eternal of eternal life, and a relationship with you. I present my body to you as a living sacrifice, and I ask you to fill me with the Holy Spirit. I pray this in Jesus' name. Amen.

The second step is to learn to hear God's voice. Hearing God begins with learning how God spoke to people in the past, and that means reading the Bible. If the Bible is new to you, I recommend reading the Gospel of Luke, the Gospel of John, and the Acts of the Apostles. If you digest these three sections of the Bible, you will have a pretty good idea about the core of Jesus' life and teachings, and the way God moves in the lives of Christians. Along with the Bible, you need to take time to listen to God individually. Get a notebook, and begin to take time to listen. Ask God to speak to you, and write these things down. Also, develop relationships with Christians, and test what God is telling you through them. It is important to make relationships with other Christians.

Our imagination is one of the most important parts of our mind. It gives us the ability to see the impossible. It helps us see the unseen. Through our imagination we are given the opportunity to be creative. This is something that reflects the personality of God more than anything else.

Our imaginations are so important that the enemy of our souls in this day has made it a major battleground for the destruction of humanity. No other time in history has it been possible to access visual images, sounds, music, or material that is negative or defiling to the imagination.

A prime example is how the public has accepted homosexuality. In the 1970's, a few television shows briefly made jokes about homosexuality, but always put it in a positive light. Slowly over time, the media has quietly repeated the message, "homosexuality is good." This whisper campaign through subtle images on television and in the movies, then through magazines and newspapers, has caused homosexuality to be generally accepted by the public. What was clearly accepted as immoral thirty years ago – and this understanding was supported by civil law – has now been accepted as a somewhat desirable "lifestyle."

Pornography and violence probably do more damage to the imagination than anything else. Both of these things become limits on the soul. There are millions of people today who have stunted or have been deadened because of their exposure to this heightened form of ugliness.

The holy imagination becomes a place where God can interface with us. When we have a cleansed imagination, we can hear the things God tells us, about ourselves, about the world, and about himself, and we can receive. Not only that, but we also begin to discover that nothing is impossible with God. Our wildest imaginations can become reality. There are no limits to what God can do if we yield ourselves to him. The Bible talks about taking every thought captive to the will of God. This is how we maintain our imaginations. Paul tells us "no eye has seen, no ear has heard, and no mind has ever conceived the glorious things that God has prepared for those who have believed."

If you feel you have defiled your imagination, you can pray the following prayer:

> *Lord Jesus, I have looked on things that are unholy, and I have been defiled by them. I know that my imagination is the platform you use to change me, and change the world. I give my imagination to you, and I ask you, by the power of the Holy Spirit, to cleanse the imaginations of my heart.*
>
> *(If images begin to appear, take your hand, and pull them out of your thoughts, keep doing this until no more appear.)*
>
> *Thank you for healing my imagination. Help me to hear, see, and do what you want me to do. Fill my imagination with a sense of the holy, the good, and the beautiful, in Jesus' name. Amen.*

May you learn to soar with God, and experience the glory he is pouring out on the earth.

If this material has been helpful to you, or you have questions, please email me at christ@belonginghouse.org.

Glory to God whose power, working in us, can do infinitely more than we can ask or imagine: Glory to him from generation to generation in the Church, and in Christ Jesus for ever and ever. Amen. (Ephesians 3:20,21)

recommended reading

LISTENING TO GOD

Blackaby, Henry and Claude King. *Experiencing God*. Nashville: Broadman & Holman Publishers, 2004.

Deere, Jack. *Surprised by the Voice of God*. Grand Rapids: Zondervan, 1996.

Joyner, Rick. *A Prophetic Vision for the 21st Century: a Spiritual Map to Help You Navigate into the Future*. Nashville: Nelson Books, 1999.

Payne, Leanne. *Listening Prayer*. Grand Rapids: Baker Books, 1999.

FAITH

Baker, Rolland and Heidi Baker. *Always Enough*. Grand Rapids: Chosen Books, 2003.

Johnson, Bill. *The Supernatural Power of a Transformed Mind*. Shippensburg: Destiny Image Publishers, 2005.

Johnson, Bill. *When Heaven Invades Earth*. Shippensburg: Treasure House, 2003.

Johnson, Bill. *Dreaming with God*. Shippensburg: Destiny Image Publishers, 2006.

Wigglesworth, Smith. *Ever Increasing Faith*. Springfield: Gospel Publishing House, 1971.

CREATIVITY

Eikleberry, Carol and Richard Bolles. *Career Guide for Creative and Unconventional People*. Berkeley: Ten Speed Press, 2007.

Elsheimer, Janice. *The Creative Call : an Artist's Response to the Way of the Spirit*. Shaw, 2001.

Wilkinson, Bruce and Heather Kopp. *The Dream Giver*. Portland: Multnomah, 2003.

HEALING AND SEXUAL SESTORATION

Comiskey, Andrew. *Pursuing Sexual Wholeness*. Orlando: Creation House, 1989.

Payne, Leanne. *The Broken Image*. Grand Rapids: Baker Books, 1996.

Payne, Leanne. *Crisis in Masculinity*. Grand Rapids: Baker Books, 1995.

Payne, Leanne. *Restoring the Christian Soul through Healing Prayer*.
Grand Rapids: Baker Books, 1996.

Prince, Derek. *Blessing or Curse*. Grand Rapids: Chosen, 2006.

Seamands, David. *Healing for Damaged Emotions*. Wheaton:
Chariot Victor Publishing, 1981.

PRAYER AND DISCIPLESHIP

Bonhoeffer, Dietrich. *The Cost of Discipleship*. New York: Scribner Paper Fiction, 1963.

Brother Lawrence. *The Practice of the Presence of God*. Garden City:
Image Books, 1977.

Buckley, Michael and Tony Castle. *The Catholic Prayer Book*. Ann Arbor:
Servant Books, 1986.

Hartley, Fred A, III. *Prayer on Fire*. Colorado Springs:
Navpress Publishing Group, 2006.

Stott, John. *Basic Christianity*. Downer's Grove: IVP Books, 2007.

CPSIA information can be obtained at www.ICGtesting.com
Printed in the USA
LVOW06s0828130713

342676LV00018BA/584/P